TOWARD A RICHER FAITH

Most of us tie our faith to a fixed set of beliefs. We tend to look upon other religions as less pure or genuine. We forget that the Oriental finds many of our beliefs incredible.

Yet no religion should be measured by its lowest expression—it should be measured by its highest. And looking at the great prophets of the great religions, we see how similar they were in many of their attitudes. To honor one does not mean to dishonor another. . . .

THE GREAT RELIGIONS

BY WHICH MEN LIVE

former title:

Questions that matter most asked by the world's religions

by

Floyd H. Ross

and

Tynette Hills

FAWCETT PREMIER • NEW YORK

A Fawcett Premier Book
Published by Ballantine Books
Copyright MCMLIV, The Beacon Press.
Copyright 1956, The Beacon Press.

THE GREAT RELIGIONS BY WHICH MEN LIVE was origi-
nally published by The Beacon Press under the title QUESTIONS
THAT MATTER MOST ASKED BY THE WORLD'S RELI-
GIONS.

ISBN 0-449-30047-1

This edition published by arrangement with The Beacon Press

Printed in Canada

First Fawcett Premier Edition: December 1956
First Ballantine Books Edition: December 1983
Twenty-first Printing: December 1990

To
FRANCES and JIM

FOREWORD

Prophets are people who live out on the fringe of their society. They are not tied down to the manners and ways of their own people but walk out where their vision takes in wider horizons. They carve out new paths. Their religion is open and outreaching.

Priests are those who minister close to the altars of convention. They are the salesmen of wares handed on to them and the distributors of tradition. They do not so much create as conserve.

All religions have their prophets and priests—few of the former and many of the latter. The institutions such as the shrine and the temple, the church and the synagogue are the concern of the priests; reform, new revelations, and fresh insights are the meat and drink of the prophets.

Christianity (like all religions) has been a religion of many facets. Down through the centuries it has had its full measure of both prophets and priests—the latter in the great majority. Most of us have been taught our religion by means of some institution, and we easily come to believe the institution's interpretation of it. We tie our faith to the faith of the church (our church), to a set of beliefs, to fixed forms and patterns. We tend to look askance upon others not of our own household—regarding others as "less pure" or less genuine. Institutional religion is by nature divisive: it sets people off from each other, sometimes deliberately (with creeds and polity) and more often unconsciously (by the nurture of pride that we are the possessors of religious truths). Priest religions are like nationalisms: self-perpetuating and self-conscious.

When we look across the borders to other religions, we

tend to look down from our self-assertive heights. We like to point out how naive and superstitious are the beliefs of people in other geographical and cultural areas, how immature their gods, how fantastic their practices. We forget that if an Oriental looked at us from his heights he would find many of our Christian practices and even our beliefs equally incredible and many of our religious manners fantastic.

It is unfair to measure any religion by its lowest expressions. All religions have their heights as well as their lowlands, and the heights are to be seen clearly in their creators, their founders, and their great literature. The measure of a religion is its best ideals. We expect others to estimate our religion by its best expression; and, in turn, as an elemental courtesy, we should judge others by their best. A Christian always prefers to have Jesus of Nazareth represent his religion when it is judged; and those of the other faiths would choose their best prophets to represent them when comparisons are made.

If our approach is in this spirit, we come to see how much alike the greater prophets in all the greater religions are as they have pointed the direction for men, how similar they are in estimating virtues, and how, presumably, their best gods show character not unlike some of the best traits we know. The metaphors of religions differ greatly. All religions thrive in metaphors appropriate to specific times, places, and cultures. But metaphors are instruments and not ends. God is always more than any metaphor.

To believe in a worthy God is to believe in a God of all people, whatever the race or clime; a God not far from consecrated human spirits anywhere.

There are many prophets of divinity, though the light may be transmitted more brightly through some than through others. To honor one of them in deepest reverence does not mean to dishonor others. We need to know more about the prophets of other great religions who presumably have transmitted divine light, even as we ought to hunger to know more about the unclouded message of the founder of our own religion. We can afford to be charitable toward those who so haltingly understood their prophets and who, as priests, have gotten lost in the coarse details of their religion.

This book, it seems to me, is a prophetic book. While it shows forth priestly religions, it sets the sights toward the prophetic in all of them. It is prophetic in its evident purpose: to stimulate a warmer appreciation of great prophets and great prophetic literature. It is prophetic in its evident desire: to promote the attitude that the sons of men must cultivate in the days ahead, while cultures are impinging upon cultures, while people are being drawn together in the interchange of communication and in the awareness of a common destiny. The way the world is going, we shall have to grow big in spirit, in tolerance and fraternity. There is hardly any other choice for survival.

It is my own belief that if the founders of the great faiths were with us today they would cross the borders that their disciples have set up between them; they would sit down at a table to express their agreements and discern the truths behind their various metaphors. They would find kinship in a common world of spirit, their common God.

Many of us are finding out how alike people are in their deepest aspirations. If you exchange ideas with a liberal of the Jewish faith, you will find him close to your own (if your own has the breath of fresh air that the prophet breathes). You will not be surprised if one of your friends calls himself both Christian and Buddhist, if you know something of the essentials of each faith. You will attend the simple service of a Ramakrishna meetinghouse in New York City with the feeling that the founder of your own religion is present in this house of God. And you will appreciate the Hindu affirmation that truth shines more brilliantly when it shines from many angles, like the diamond with its many facets. You will be impressed by the counsel of the Hindu who urges you, not to give up your own religious heritage, but to see it with the help of its greatest prophet rather than the dogmas of its priests.

Dr. Ross is eminently qualified to point the way to a larger faith. Professor of World Religions at the University of Southern California, he is the author of *The Meaning of Life in Hinduism and Buddhism* and *Addressed to Christians: Isolationism vs. World Community*, and co-author of *Ethics and the Modern World*. He knows his own historic religion intimately, and his studies have brought him closer to the prophets and prophetic literature of other great religions.

Mrs. Hills has been a public-school teacher and a member of the religious-education staffs of several large churches. After majoring in religion at the University of Southern California, she went on to study for her M.A. degree there.

Together they have produced a book that points in the right direction for the days immediately ahead.

VERGILIUS FERM

The College of Wooster
Wooster, Ohio

ACKNOWLEDGMENTS

THE AUTHORS wish to express their appreciation for the assistance of Sophia L. Fahs in the editing of the total manuscript. Jeanette Perkins Brown made helpful suggestions on earlier drafts. Rabbi Edwin Zerin went over the material on Judaism and made valuable comments. And Professor Paul Irwin of the School of Religion, University of Southern California, made many pertinent suggestions regarding the over-all planning.

CONTENTS

INTRODUCTION

1. We Look at Life

A STORY is told of three men who were shipwrecked on an island in the South Seas. As the ship was pounded to pieces on the coral shoals, food, clothing, and equipment were lost in the surf. The three exhausted survivors pulled themselves up on the beach out of reach of the pounding waves. Having caught their breath, they began to take stock of their surroundings. Beyond the sandy stretch arose wooded hills and then rocky ledges and steep precipices. There was no evidence of any human being aside from themselves. The only sounds were the roaring of the ocean and the noisy cries of the gulls.

Not one of the men had a compass. Their radio had been lost in the wreck. Their immediate urge was to find out whether the island was inhabited. The food supply, they saw, would be no problem, for tropical fruits abounded. But they desperately wanted to find out where they were. They realized that this meant making a search for other persons who might be able to give them a clue as to their whereabouts. It was decided that one man would work along the beach in one direction, a second man going in the opposite direction. The third man was to penetrate to the foothills. Each sought some sign of human habitation—a footprint, a cultivated field, or smoke from some village in the distance.

In the hours of search that followed, it was the third man who discovered the first trace of human beings—smoke rising from a small hut high up on a mountain side. He reported back to his companions, and all three set off for the village. The islanders proved to be quite friendly. Before many weeks were past, the men found passage on a small boat, which took them in the direction of their homeland.

Our Island Universe

You and I are in a similar situation. Without choice we have been cast up on this "island" called Earth. Like shipwrecked men, we can either feel terribly sorry for ourselves or start looking around to try to get our bearings. To be sure, we do not have to search for people, for we are usually surrounded by them. However, we sometimes find it difficult to locate people who can help us find out exactly where we are or assist us toward our destination.

As children, we take for granted that our parents know all the answers. As we get older we sometimes try to solve our problems in the same ways our parents seem to have solved theirs. We sometimes forget that they cannot know all the answers to all life's problems. They live on the island, too. And nobody asked them if they wanted to be here. Finding themselves here, they set out to make the best of it. They have found some answers through their living.

We are guided in our early years by their learned wisdom, partial though it is. But we cannot safely guide our lives solely by the ideas of those who have happened to live ahead of us. Nor can we accept their suggestions blindly. We must remember that an answer can be ours only when we have made it a part of our experience. No parent or teacher can live for us. There is much we can learn only through living and learning for ourselves.

Can We Be Honest with Ourselves?

Some people appear to be living day by day without taking much time to think about it. They never seem to wonder about the world in which they live or their place in it. Their living is controlled by habit, and they do not seem to look for any improvements. It is unfortunate when this happens to anyone, for he is losing his opportunity to grow and progress. The continuing search for better answers about the nature of life and the universe adds zest to living. It is much more thrilling than having to accept old answers and customs and habits just because they are old.

A person may stop wondering and questioning because some adult discouraged him. Sometimes teachers and parents are too tired, too busy, or too impatient to give helpful attention to a younger person's questions. So he just quits asking after a time. Others become so interested in social activities or sports or work that they ignore their deeper wonderings about the nature of things.

Yet the questions are there inside us. What is life? How did we get here? What is God like? What is the difference between right and wrong? What is love? What happens to us when we die? These and many other questions like them have been asked by people of all lands and all times.

If we are honest with ourselves, we let such questions absorb some of our attention and our efforts. Searching for answers is the way we learn. We should never feel ashamed to raise questions. Nor should we feel that someone else, no matter how famous he is, has found all the answers for us already. In order to live fully, all of us must ask about the meaning of life and try to find some satisfactory answers. Doubts and questions are healthy signs of honesty with ourselves and are a measure of our effort to increase self-understanding.

Does Religion Have "The Answers"?

Some people talk about religion as though it had all the answers, but the claim only raises more questions. What is "religion"? Is it going to church, singing songs, listening to prayers, learning how to pray? When people talk about God, what do they mean? Where do people get their ideas of God? How do we know whether they are right or not? Why should we feel that we have to believe in a certain way?

No religion has all the answers, no matter what ministers or priests may sometimes say. All religions try to raise the questions that matter most. Religions also provide a record of how some people have answered these basic questions. Many persons think that their own religion offers the best answers to everyone's questioning. But the wisest teachers of the religions have not said so. Instead, they have encouraged others to explore the meaning of life, as they themselves were doing.

What Can We Learn from Others?

As we look for the answers to our wonderings, it is often helpful to look beyond ourselves. Many people of other cultures and religions have found some important clues to the meaning of life. Their ideas may furnish us with some valuable suggestions. A study of them will give us more help than the study of one "answer" alone—exclusively that of our own nation or our own religion. It will offer us a shorter path towards the wisdom that others have gathered.

We must choose carefully the people to whom we go for help, for life does not allow us time to quiz all of our ancestors and examine all the religions of other generations. We must choose persons who have tried to be honest in the quest. We do not want to waste our time with insincere or self-important teachers, ancient or modern.

Neither do we want to get lost on a slumming expedition among the people whose religions we are going to study. If we want to discover whether Beethoven wrote music that we might like, we need to listen to his symphonies or sonatas. We should not worry over the fact that he often went around with egg stains on his tie. In the same way, if we want to find helpful suggestions from other people, we need to examine their ideas about life. We should not become preoccupied with the ways in which their clothing or customs differ from ours.

Scientists, artists, engineers, teachers, philosophers, and theologians—all, regardless of race, language, or country, are trying to find new meanings about life. Someday we may have a much more complete picture than we now have. At the moment it is as though we are still trying to put together a big jigsaw puzzle. Some people are working on one corner of the puzzle, some on another, and so on. Many of us get so interested in the tiny details that we forget the total picture. Only in our more imaginative moments do we try to get a glimpse of the whole of life. Almost always people have looked to their religions for some sense of the whole picture of life, even though countless pieces have not yet been fitted into the puzzle. Perhaps we shall learn a few things from other religions that may help us to understand more.

Why Should We Study Life at All?

As children we were very concerned with the immediate activities of every day. But as young persons we begin to discover that, while separate activities are important, they are but a part of our whole lives. And our lives are part of something much bigger—the life in which all beings share. We become more concerned about what each life is and how it relates to every other. We begin to explore the meaning of life. We are interested in doing more independent thinking than we have done before.

Our lives become increasingly a matter of our own making, and if we think about it, we make our lives meaningful. Because men everywhere have found that the meaningful life was a goal of all people, they have developed religions to help them decide what is really important. The world's religions have much to offer to us today in our personal quest for meanings and answers. All men's searches for right relationships to themselves, to others, and to the world are part of that common search in which we too are involved.

Let us take up the challenge of this quest for meaningful life, raising our questions and searching constantly and gladly for answers we can accept. As we do, we shall gain inspiration from those who have asked and answered in other times and places. Let us see what they have to say to us, and let us use what will help us to continue our search for better ways to live.

Section One

BRAHMANIC HINDUISM

2. The Unity of Life

THOUSANDS of years ago, the people of India, young and old, were wondering about the same questions that concern us today. Sometimes they tried to guess where human beings came from and where they would go after this life. They questioned further, too, even as we do. How was the world created, and how does it keep going? What is the purpose of the world? What is the difference between right and wrong? What am I? What is my place in the world? How can I really find myself?

Over the centuries, the Indians kept up the search for answers to their questions, constantly studying and interpreting their experiences in living. Each generation gave the next some suggestions about the best kind of life and the best ways of living in the universe. Later, the people decided that some of these suggestions ought to be written down, in order that they might not be forgotten or changed, as was sometimes unwittingly done in the telling. The written suggestions became the scriptures of the Hindu religion. Some of them are so old that no one knows when they were first offered as possible answers to the questions of men.

The oldest ones are ancient poems and hymns, called the *Vedas*, which are considered to be as much as 3000 years old. The *Brahmanas*—rules which the priests gave for rituals of worship—date from between 1200 and 1000 B.C. The *Upanishads*, dating from about 800 B.C., are answers that the renowned hermit-teachers of that period gave to questions about life and the universe. The *Great Epics* are philosophical and religious poems about legendary heroes and gods. They were ancient stories that had been told for generations before they were finally set down in writing at about the first century B.C. A short section of one of the *Epics*, the *Bhagavad Gita*, has become the favorite religious text in India.

If you could see all these scriptures together, you would see that the Hindu "bible" is much longer than the Bibles of Christians and Jews. Although the Hindu texts have

22

been translated into English from the original Sanskrit writing, probably there would be parts of them that you could not understand without a Hindu's explanation. Many of them would be interesting to you, for they contain stories and suggestions which attempt to answer the questions that men of today are still asking, in India and in America.

The stories in these books reveal a great deal about the Indian people who were searching for answers. For example, they reveal that the Indians valued wisdom. Among them were great students—not in the sense of those who do assigned lessons in a school, for they did not have schools such as ours. Their students were men who studied and interpreted the things that went on around them, and in so doing, they became wise. The common people observed that the wise men seemed to be most successful in living. They did not become upset with trivial things, and neither did they have to go looking feverishly for ways to be happy. They were content—at home with themselves. Since this seemed to the people to be the only true and lasting happiness they saw achieved, the man who had wisdom became a kind of national hero.

Wisdom was valued so much that the people went to great lengths to achieve it. There is one Indian story about a rich man who took much of his wealth—1000 cows, expensive jewelry, a carriage with many mules, and even his own daughter—to pay a renowned sage to teach him the meaning of life. The Indians describe a man without wisdom as being like a frog in a dried-up pond, or like a fish out of water.

A story in the Upanishads tells about an unhappy young man who came to study under the direction of a wise teacher. The teacher first asked him what he already knew. The young man responded with the titles of all the books he had read and the passages he had memorized. Then he added sadly, "I know all this, but I do not know myself. I am unhappy. Please help me to overcome this unhappiness." The teacher agreed to help, pointing out that the trouble was that the boy was trying to find wisdom in knowing words about life, instead of seeking meaning in living. So for awhile, under the tutelage of his teacher, the boy studied and meditated upon himself and his reactions to daily experiences. He became much happier and, at the end of a period of such study, felt that he was wise enough to continue his search alone.

Who Am I?

What was the happiness which the boy found through self-study and which so many Hindus seek diligently today? It was the same thing they observed in their wisest men—that at-homeness with themselves. We all know at least one person who never seems to be quite able to settle down to one thing for very long. He is always looking for something new and more exciting to do next. Another person we know appears poised in almost any place he finds himself. He seems to carry his contentment deep within. The Hindus would unanimously say that the second of our friends is the happier, for he knows himself better.

Like the unhappy young student, all people are discontented when they know just facts or just books or just things. Happiness can come only from knowing yourself. What does it mean to be yourself? Who are you? First, there is the "you" that people see and hear: the way you look, your voice, your mannerisms, your talents. Is that you? The Hindus answer that you are more than that. If you see your image in a mirror, or hear a transcription of your voice, or see yourself in a home movie, you agree with them. You are more than that.

In addition to the parts of your personality that people see and hear, there is your temperamental make-up. The Hindus have said that there are three general levels of temperament. The lowest level is inertia, unwillingness to change, or laziness. The second is aggressiveness and the capacity to be agitated by external forces. The third and best is tranquillity of spirit and the ability to remain undisturbed by outside forces. Each person has a little of each of these in his make-up. The aim is to eliminate inertia and aggressiveness from your temperament so that you may be calm and tranquil.

This is similar to the recent American emphasis on peace of mind. People are much happier when they are not disturbed by every little upsetting event. They can study and know themselves better when they have an unruffled temperament. And they will make no progress at all toward true happiness until they are willing to expand the necessary effort.

If you have ever taken the time to look inside yourself and try to explore what is there, you will realize that the things we have mentioned are not all there is to you. You have certain attitudes toward yourself, and these are part of yourself. Whether you are proud or ashamed most of the time, whether you look forward to or dread the rest of your life, whether you do more right things or more wrong things according to your own standards—these things help to form your feelings about yourself. According to the Hindus, your feelings about yourself arise from the way you look and talk and from your temperament. These feelings and the facts from which they arise form what we shall call the "outer self."

Besides the outer self, there is an essential self which you must know in order to be really happy. This very important inner self is the *Atman*. It is extremely difficult for anyone to help you understand exactly how to know the *Atman*. This is because only you can know your own inner self completely. Hindu teachers have given a few hints to help one in his search for self-knowledge. They have said that, since the *Atman* is the inner spirit of a man, it underlies all the fleeting experiences of life. It remains as the unchanging, permanent substance of you. All the qualities that make up the outer self are collected around the center core, the *Atman*, and are affected by it. But the *Atman* is not affected by them.

Some very wonderful things happen when a person succeeds in knowing what is basic and essential in himself. He learns that the everyday affairs, which may formerly have bothered him very much, are not really so important. This is because he has learned that the real center of his life is not affected by them. He learns to take a longer view of his experiences. He has perspective on life. He becomes unprejudiced and less emotional. He is able to make choices and to judge events maturely, because he is not blinded by his own emotions and attitudes. Hindus say that he has taken the most important step toward the most important human attribute—wisdom.

What Is Real?

At the same time that the Hindus were exploring the question of what the real self is, they were wondering about their world. What kind of world is it? What was the power that had created the world and still made it continue? They looked about them and saw the trees, the mountains, the plains, and the rivers. They felt the rain and the wind. They came to know all the other living creatures with whom they shared the land.

They realized that they could not say that the world was any one of these. Nor was it just the total of the things they saw and felt and knew. The world was more than all these things. The power that had made the world and made it continue was indeed more than the things in the world. But the world, they decided, was an evidence of that power, just as they themselves were. Everything in the whole universe, including themselves, was a result of the working of the creative and continuing force. All things were kin, then, because all had the same origin.

Thoughts such as these made them conclude that there is a fundamental unity of all existence and all experience. A Hindu will tell us that all apparent differences which people think so important are trivial and temporary. They seem for a time to be important, but soon they fade away or change. For example, all of us can distinguish between a living being and the elements of the earth. Yet, in death, all living beings return to the elements. There are no exceptions. The Hindu who points to such illustrations is trying to say that in the very beginning there was unity (no differences). In the end, there will also be unity. It is just a matter of time.

In the *Rig Veda*, there is the Hindu Hymn of Creation, which tries to explain how the world came to be. This hymn stresses that there was unity in the beginning, and no distinctions could be made:

Existence was not, nor its opposite,
Nor earth, nor heaven's blue vault, nor aught beyond.

Death was not yet, nor deathlessness; the day
Was night, night day, for neither day nor night
Had come to birth.

The hymn goes on to tell about the power behind the world:

Then THAT, the primal fount
Of light — immobile — rest and action joined —
Brooded in silent bliss. Itself beside,
In the wide universe there nothing was.

The important thing that the hymn emphasizes is the supreme unity of THAT (or THAT ONE), the ALL which lies behind or beyond both existence and non-existence. In THAT, there are no differences. Rest and action are joined, for example. Everything is united.

The Hindus use THAT to refer to the supreme One, *Brahman*. They use the neuter pronoun in order to avoid any idea of a manlike God or Creator or First Principle. They believe that *Brahman* is the ultimate reality behind and beyond all the things that men find to be "real" from experiencing them through the senses.

This is a different idea about God from that of most Christians and Jews. Many use the term "God" to mean a personalized God—that is, a God who has characteristics like a person. For example, we are familiar with expressions like, "God loves," "God is merciful," "the face of God," "the hand of God." Hindus say that such personal descriptions are qualities people admire in other people. And since they believe that God is infinitely good, people surmise that God has unlimited amounts of these admirable qualities. But, say the Hindus, God—if we use that term to mean the REALITY and the true nature of the universe—is beyond such human representation. And that is what they mean by *Brahman*, or THAT.

In the Hindu religion, there are personal gods to be worshiped by those persons who so desire. Often it is these gods about which we are told most in writings on Hinduism. According to Hindu myths, the gods have wives (who are also worshiped), and they live almost like human beings. Out of a large number of gods, three are worshiped most by present-day Hindus. The three together form a Hindu trinity: *Brahma*, the creator; *Vishnu*, the savior; *Shiva*, the destroyer and restorer.

Hindus believe that the creation of the world is a continuing thing in which men share, not something that happened long ago in the past. Therefore, they believe that the three gods work to carry out the continual creation. At the end of each cycle or age in creation, Shiva destroys the old world. Brahma creates a new world. When, during the cycle, men face a problem they cannot solve alone, Vishnu comes as a human being or in some other form, with special powers to give the necessary aid.

The many other gods and goddesses are also worshiped

in whatever ways the people see fit, with prayers, praise, and gifts. Devotees appeal to them to attend to and to bless all phases of human life. And yet, even while they worship the personal gods, the educated Hindus know that the gods are essentially human ideals that men imagine to be objective reality. They do not actually exist in the form in which the people think they exist. The real function of the worship of personal gods is to direct the worshiper to knowledge of Brahman, which lies beyond all men's wondering and speculation about the universe.

One can always raise that most troublesome of all questions: "Why was a world created at all?" To this men have not found a final answer, according to the Hindus. Their Hymn of Creation mentions it:

Ah, vain are words, and weak all mortal thought!
Who is there truly knows, and who can say,
Whence this unfathomed world, and from what cause?
Nay, even the gods were not! Who, then, can know?

The source from which this universe hath sprung,
That source, and that alone, can bear it up —
None else: THAT, THAT alone, lord of the worlds,
In its own self contained, immaculate
As are the heavens above, THAT alone knows
The truth of what itself hath made — none else!

But if men cannot know the reasons for the creation of the world, they can know something more important. They can know Brahman. The Hindu scriptures are full of suggestions about how a person may live his own life in order to experience the essential unity that is the pattern of all creation. When you know the Atman, your own "inner self," you also know the heart of the universe, Brahman, the "inner self" of all creation. A person can know Brahman only by knowing himself. Hindus say, "He who knows himself will know God."

One of their scripture readings describes it in this way:

The spirit within me is smaller than a mustard seed.
The spirit within me is greater than this earth and
sky and the heaven and all these united. It is Brahman.

Happiness lies in the direction of finding real meanings: the real self, the real nature of the universe. Brahman expresses itself in many ways—in man, through the *Atman*. But *Brahman* is not one of the expressions: THAT is beyond them all. When a man truly knows the *Atman*, then he may know *Brahman*. When he knows both, he sees that *Atman* and *Brahman* are united. And man realizes the supreme knowledge, gains the supreme happiness. All the creatures and creations of the earth are the same, bound up in inclusive *Brahman*. There is no diversity, no real difference in any part of reality. All are the same. All are one. "It is *Brahman*."

3. What Is My Place in This Universe?

W<small>HY</small> can't I be happy?

Why do I make so many mistakes?

Why am I so often afraid?

These are the questions people often ask themselves and others when they are thinking about the ways they live their lives. For thousands of years, men of every race and nationality have offered seemingly good explanations for ways to be happy. Yet, persons in every generation and in every land live unhappy and sometimes worthless lives—by their own confession.

Hindus say that one of the biggest reasons for man's unhappiness is maya. Each person born into this world suffers from confusion and finds it difficult to know the important things in his experience because of maya. The world is maya in the sense that it is always changing from what it is into something else that changes and so on without ceasing. No man can know what the world is, for the world never is: that is, it never stands still long enough to be studied and explained; it is always becoming. Therefore, men easily become bewitched into attaching great importance to something that in reality is trivial.

Hindus do not mean that the world is not important, but they emphasize the fact that the world as we see it is not the real world. It continually confuses us. For example, if you look down a straight stretch of railroad tracks on a level roadbed, you will see the tracks meet in the distance. Actually they do not meet, but to you they appear to do so.

The eye, the hand, the ear, the touch—all deceive us again and again. How can we be so sure that the world we "know" through our first-hand experience is the real world? We cannot be sure, answers the Hindu. Because we are so often confused by apparent truth, we must learn to interpret all our experiences, in order to find reality.

No matter how carefully wise men explained the danger of confusion because of maya and the importance of knowing Atman and Brahman, there were still some people who lived miserable lives. The Hindus were concerned about these unhappy people. Why did this happen? How could it be prevented? They wondered about such things as the inequality in abilities between persons, the inequalities in joy and pain. They wanted a reasonable explanation.

They decided that it did not make much sense to say that it was all a matter of accident or chance, or that *Brahman* was responsible for the inequalities. That would make *Brahman* unfair and arbitrary. It did not satisfy the questioners to say that all the differences would be solved in some eternity of "heaven" or "hell," because people did not seem to fall into two distinct groups of "good" and "bad."

Hindus found a satisfactory answer in a belief in reincarnation (or transmigration). Each person has had many lives and will go on having many lives—enough to discover who he really is. Life is a school to a man; in it he comes to know *Atman* and *Brahman*. When he attains this knowledge, he leaves the school of life. He does not need to enroll again; he has "passed the course."

Life is described by the Hindus as being like a stream or river, which flows ceaselessly, without beginning and without ending. All things are part of this stream of existence: stones, plants, animals, men, and so on. Everything exists in life after life until it has come to knowledge of the unity of *Atman* and *Brahman*. Each will have as many opportunities for coming to self-knowledge as he needs. This doctrine of reincarnation offers hope to all. No one will be punished for an unlimited period because of a limited number of mistakes.

There is a universal law which operates throughout all life. Whatever is sown must be reaped sometime and somewhere. This is the law: every action, every intention to act, every attitude bears its own fruit. "A man becomes good by good deeds and bad by bad deeds," says one of the Hindu sacred writings. This means that each person is really responsible for his own condition, whether he is confused and mixed-up and unhappy—or happy. We may want to put the blame on someone else, perhaps our parents. Or we may wish to carry it back to our grandparents or even to *Brahman*. But this is avoiding the real issue. You are what you are because of what you have done in the past. To a Hindu the past, of course, would include all previous lives or existences. Each person can break with that past only by stretching his mind and gaining knowledge of his real self.

The Indian writings emphasize that one must exert himself to know the *Atman* if the influence of past unhappiness is to be outgrown or cast off. But a person very often does not make this his goal. He ignores his real nature, and this is the chief evil from which he suffers. He is blind to his real capacities. Many of us sink into the rut of habit and let our past actions and attitudes govern the way we react to present situations instead of aspiring to higher goals. This is like a mountain climber who fails to reach his goal because in his fear of the heights he forgets his real desire to climb the mountain.

Many people live without thinking about it and simply react the way they always have. Hindus describe them as "rushing about like one possessed by an evil spirit; bitten by the world like one bitten by a great serpent." When a person finds himself running around in this distracted way, he should stop and remind himself, "This is not my true nature." Sometimes people do things which they themselves cannot understand. "Why did I do that?" one asks himself later. Sometimes it is as though a closet door in our insides had suddenly burst open and things we had stuck inside came tumbling out before we could stop them. Sometimes such internal explosions are accompanied by a great deal of emotional expression: we get angry, we get sad, we become moody, we have tantrums. Such actions are not the result of intelligent choice, but of the load of past attitudes and actions we carry with us. The way to overcome both *maya* and the influence of the past is to stop and ask, "But what is the real Me? What is the *Atman?*"

Caste and Duty

According to the Hindu teachings, every person has a specific place in life and specific responsibilities. Each person is born where he is, and with particular abilities that he has, because of past actions and attitudes. This underlies the whole pattern of society in India, and it includes what is known as *caste*. There are four main castes, mentioned in some of the Hindu writings. These are: (1) the intellectual-priestly group; (2) the nobility, including the warriors; (3) the administrative group, including merchants and landowners; and (4) the great masses of people who do the common work of a society. The class of so-called "untouchables" or "out-castes" (recently abolished by Indian law) was composed of people who had originally belonged to different sub-groups of the fourth caste, the masses. Through various social and economic conditions, they "lost caste," or lost their place in society.

Within the four castes, there are dozens of sub-divisions. Through the years, more than a thousand levels of castes have appeared in Indian social life; but all belong to one of the four main groups. In ordinary social life, caste lines have frequently reflected real injustices and strong preju-dices. Many thoughtful Hindus today realize that abuses have crept into the system. In the twentieth century, many efforts have been made in the direction of straightening out some of the gross injustices. Gandhi was one who gave freely of his energies in restoring the "untouchables" to caste status.

The caste system serves to afford each person a particu-lar niche in society, with certain duties to be performed in the best way he can. Just as no person can be someone else, neither can he pull himself out of one caste in this life and enter another. In successive rebirths, he can better his position—if he does his present task well. It is also taught in India that even the lowest caste members may attain complete knowledge of the *Atman*, if they try hard enough. They can in that way attain the greatest fulfill-ment life has to offer.

4. What Shall My Life Goals Be?

OVER AND OVER again, another question arose in the minds of the Indians: "What is my life for?" or "What should I do with my life?" Thoughtful Hindus came to believe that there are four basic goals, which include all valuable parts of human activity and give purpose to every life.

The most important goal for each person to achieve is release from the influence of past unhappiness. Each person has the fundamental aim all through life of escaping from maya through union with Brahman. To help the person in the process of reaching this goal, there are other lesser goals to be fulfilled along the way.

One of these is the life of pleasure, fulfillment of all normal human desires, including the very important desires rooted in sex. Hindus do not reject the sensory experiences of life—development of creative relationships with other people, aesthetic appreciation, sexual expression. The Hindus value these experiences when used correctly and not regarded as the only goals of life. The life of pleasure is included as one of the four goals of men.

Another human goal is participation in economic activity or public welfare, which includes working in some worthwhile job or profession. Each person has an obligation to himself and to society to do some useful work. For this he receives the wherewithal for his daily needs, and through it he contributes to the common welfare. A person's economic responsibility to the community is not to be ignored as of no importance, for it is one of the four life goals.

The fourth important achievement for each Hindu is living the right kind of moral or ethical life. One has a duty to himself and to others to do what is expected of him morally and ethically. The duty has been rather specifically defined in India, for each caste has a code of actions and attitudes which are expected of its members. And to this code a person is pledged through all his endeavors if he wishes to attain the good life.

Large segments of Hindu teachings have been concerned with the idea of moral duty. Since Hindus stress the unity of all existence, they believe that one person is important to all other persons. This means that each must learn to rise above his own selfish interests. When deciding what to do, most people are tempted to say: "What am I going to gain from this?" Hindus say that we find lasting happiness when we do a thing because for us in our situation it is the right thing, regardless of the gain we receive.

"To work and work alone are you entitled, not to its fruits. Desire for the fruits of work must never be your motive in working. . . . Wretched are they who work for results." Thus reads a statement in one of their sacred texts.

We often say somewhat the same thing in noting that he who plays a game because he loves to play it is happier than he who plays to win. The more intent one is upon winning the game, the more he loses what the playing of the game can offer him. On the other hand, if one plays the game for the sake of the playing, the results take care of themselves. Win or lose, he will have had the satisfaction of playing. The Hindus say that it is the same with all of life's activities. The important thing is how we feel about what we do and the way we do it—not what we gain from it.

The Stages of Life

The ancient Hindus knew that there were certain periods in a person's life when one goal could be more easily sought than at other times. They divided life into several stages, and then they tried to point out what pleasures or actions were appropriate for each stage. Instruction in the four goals was to be given according to the individual's readiness to learn about them and his ability to achieve them at that time.

For example, the child does not need to worry about his later economic and ethical obligations to society. He will have time to learn about them as he grows older. Neither is a child ready for an adult religious experience. Therefore, it would be foolish to expect him to achieve those adult goals. Persons whose duty to caste codes requires them to devote a great deal of time and effort to economic activity are not expected to be very concerned about that most important goal of union of Atman and Brahman. This is true of the lowest caste group, the workers. However, Indians have never claimed the members of the lowest caste cannot realize such a union in their present lifetimes. It simply is not expected of them, because they are required to be so busy with other responsibilities.

All male members of the three higher castes are advised to follow the suggested life plan, whereby they might attain all the goals. The ancient teachers who developed the plan emphasized the importance of studying and interpreting life. In following the plan, a man will become in successive stages a student, a householder, a retired man, and a spiritual pilgrim.

The Student Stage. The length of time spent in this stage varies, depending upon the particular caste to which one belongs. Every young man of the upper castes is expected to live for a time with his religious tutor who teaches him the ancient wisdom of India and directs his reading of the sacred books. Each student is personally helped to learn the meaning of life and is encouraged to find his proper place in it.

According to tradition, no young man in the student phase of his life is supposed to marry. In modern India, however, many of the old customs are not followed as strictly as formerly. Today, some marriages do occur before the young man has completed the usual student phase —but they are comparatively few in number. Many Indian parents still choose the wives for their sons. Since the arrangements are made by the parents of the couple, usually when they are both quite young, the young man is not expected to take time from his studies to court his future wife.

In general, there is no social custom comparable to the dating done in the United States today. The adults do not pretend that young people are not interested in the opposite sex. They simply arrange that the interest will not be unduly aroused before the young people are ready for the responsibilities of children. For the three higher castes, this usually means after the young men have passed through the student phases of their lives. Indian law now requires that a girl must be at least fifteen years of age before she can marry; the boy may not be married before eighteen.

There are reasons why the student stage is important

enough to be completed. Every person has a natural capacity to wonder about life and to raise questions about it. Many of those questions are so big that no person has ever found more than a partial answer, but people seem somehow driven to keep trying to find answers, to learn and continue to learn. The student stage promotes this learning process.

According to Hindus, it also gives one a chance to get what they call his "second birth." The first birth was an event over which one had no control, but the second birth is in part an achievement resulting from one's own efforts. The Indians call it a spiritual rebirth: a young person begins to see something of the meaning of life. It is essential that one catch the meaning of life before he assumes family obligations.

The Householder Stage. Although one should retain the student's desire to learn, he cannot remain forever with a teacher. Soon the former student is expected to marry and undertake the responsibilities of parenthood. In the householder stage, the Hindu can attain three of the four goals of life. He can find the meaning of the life of pleasure, for the marriage relationship should help to release all the basic human energies and drives. Being a member of the family requires that the person make his own contribution to the economic stability of society by productive work. And certainly the householder has opportunities to do his duty according to the ethical code of his caste. If India has changed slowly through the years, it is because of the specific rights and duties that were regarded as binding on each person in each caste.

The Retired Stage. The three goals that can be attained in the householder stage of life are important. But they should contribute to a larger goal—the finding of the real self and the real nature of the universe. Therefore, the Hindus provided for a third step, retirement from public life, at which time a man (and his wife with him, if they so wish it) might return to student interests. After one's first grandchild is born, one is permitted to withdraw from business or professional activities, give up direct family responsibilities, and retire to a forest hermitage for study. In a group of like-minded retired persons, the middle-aged student now has the opportunity to push further than in his student days the questions: What is the meaning of life? What am I? What is God like?

Not everyone in India can go on to this stage. Members of the upper castes normally have a better chance to do so because of the more favorable economic conditions which are theirs. People in Indian live in large family groups instead of in single-family units as Americans usually do. If one man leaves the large family compound, he is not missed as badly as he would be in a single family plan. Even in America, some people retire from business after the children are married. In India, a man who retires does so not only from business but also from the usual daily activities of the householder or family stage. He has outgrown the need for the earlier kinds of amusement and activities. He wants to reflect, to study, to meditate.

The Stage of Spiritual Pilgrim. There is a fourth stage that can be undertaken—but few enter into it. If he feels ready to do so, a man may leave his hermitage, his village, his group of congenial friends. Taking his staff and begging bowl, he wanders from place to place without cares or worries—eating whatever comes his way through the grace of those dwelling in the villages through which he travels. He helps the people by sharing his wisdom about the meaning of life or merely by his presence. He may live for a while as the tutor of a young student; but when he finishes the task, he wanders off again.

Westerners have frequently scorned this ideal. Yet, as Indians who know the story of Jesus point out, Jesus was demanding something like this of his own immediate followers. They were to give up everything—including family obligations—in order to follow him. To those who were ready for the step, he gave the invitation: leave everything. The search for meaning is more important than any institution—even the family. The wandering Hindu pilgrim is expressing this conviction dramatically when he leaves every vestige of his former life, in full dedication to the attempt to understand the real self. The attempt may result in physical hardship and loneliness, but the Hindu pilgrim believes these to be unimportant, for the Atman lies beyond comfort and companionship.

Hinduism teaches us that we can find the real self only if we search honestly. The search starts during our student days. It goes on through our family days and our retired days. The search does not involve giving up anything that is natural. One should not try to repress or suppress part of his life, his feelings, or his emotions. One should try to see all the desires, urges, and feelings for what they are.

Facing these honestly, a person discovers many things about himself. When he discovers what he himself is, he discovers what he is most capable of doing. Doing that with all of his heart just because he wants to do it, and doing it with love, he discovers that he is worshiping. To worship God is at the same time to find the real self and its meaning. These values are to be found only by the person who, with the honest desire to learn the answers to his basic questions, plans and lives his life for fulfillment of his highest goals.

5. How Shall I Worship?

THE simple folk of Hindu India have listened for many centuries to the advice of their scholars and their wise men. They have heard the answers these learned ones gave to the questions about life and its meaning. And they have done their best to adopt the answers as their own. But there are many people in India, as elsewhere, who cannot make religion their main business. They must till the soil for food for their families and for other people—for even priests must eat. There are some who must tend the shops, or else all commerce would cease. There are women, whom many men still consider to be incapable of gaining the knowledge that the wise philosophers considered essential.

What are these people to do? They wish to have happy lives. They wish to live at their best. Above all, they wish to free themselves of the endless chain of reincarnations, which, they fear, will keep them living life after life of work and worry. Is there some way that these people may come to know the Great Power within the universe, without having to spend all their days seeking? Is there some way they can live in accordance with the universal laws, without having to spend the money and the time to study with a wise teacher?

The Help of Gods and Goddesses

To people like these, *Brahman* is difficult to understand. *Brahman* seems vast and remote. To these people the world seems much more friendly if they have a personal god "on their side." They want some god to pray to, to give gifts to, to honor in special ceremonies. They feel that such a god will help them to success in their material understakings and in their spiritual lives. Because the wise men said that everything reflects *Brahman*, the people consider their god or goddess to be divine. And many of the people feel that a god like this is all of *Brahman* they need to know.

And so over the centuries, some personal gods have come to be very popular with the Hindu people. Of the

Hindu trinity, Shiva (the destroyer-restorer god) and Vishnu (the savior god) are especially revered. (Vishnu is most often worshiped in one of his incarnated forms, Rama or Krishna.) Worshipers seek the aid of the wives of the gods, too. Some of the important goddesses are Durga, Lakshmi, Sita, and Radha. The most famous is Kali, the Mother Goddess of India. Many temples are built in her honor, and she is worshiped as the universal mother and feared as the foe of all sinful people.

There are many less-known deities to whom shrines are erected and to whom prayers and offerings are given. Among these are animal gods, nature gods, and legendary heroes. A count of the gods worshiped in India would yield a figure of several hundreds. Each family chooses one god or goddess to worship in particular. While the members of the family may pray and give offerings to other gods, they never forget to pay daily reverence to the family god at the home shrine.

Such gods and goddesses seem closer to men than Brahman, for they are thought to understand human failings and human hopes. So a visitor to India sees images of various gods being fed and dressed and taken for walks. For all of these activities there are suitable rituals, hymns, and prayers. There is somewhere in Hinduism a deity that the humblest of men can comfortably worship.

In this way the masses of Hindu believers answer their questions about what the world is like and what the power behind it is. When they see a storm, they believe it to be the work of one of their gods. When they begin a new undertaking, they believe another of the gods will help them. To some, the world has almost "come alive" with gods and goddesses who can be loved or appeased.

What the average Hindu wants most is aid in his life's pilgrimage. He believes that he can expect to go on living in one body after another until he learns enough about the true nature of himself and about life. And since he knows he cannot spend as much time as the sages and priests in meditation and study, he looks for short cuts to help him. He hopes to find ways that will give him special merit with the gods—especially Kali, Vishnu, and Shiva. He believes that since the gods are reflections of the Supreme Spirit, Brahman, the person who so worships is truly helped.

A great number of short cuts have been developed by

Hindu devotees. That is the reason travelers to India return with stories strange to our ears. They tell of people thronging to bathe in the River Ganges, the largest river there, and in other rivers and streams. Hindus come to the water because they believe it to be especially purifying; it will wash away some of their past sins and give them merit with the gods. Even the river banks are considered sacred. Some Hindus hope to gain ease for their consciences or a better position in their next lives by walking for great distances along the banks of some of the rivers.

The city of Benares is a sacred city to Hindus. They believe that a person who dies within a ten-mile radius of the city will have the mistakes of his previous lives forgotten by the gods. He may go for a stay of many years in one of the heavens of which Hindus speak. But after this "rest" from the plan of transmigration, he must return to earth to live out the lives necessary for him to gain complete self-knowledge and *Brahman*-knowledge.

Through centuries of search for merit, the Hindu believers have added other religious customs. The cow is treated as a holy animal, and prayers are addressed to it. Monkeys must never be harmed, for they, too, are sacred. Some plants are addressed with prayers. The wise men of India explain this by saying that the *Atman* is present in every living thing. Some nearby animal might be the present life of the *Atman* that used to be housed by a relative of yours in an earlier life.

Gandhi—called by his compatriots the *Mahatma* or "Great Soul"—said that cow-worship was the distinctive contribution of Hinduism to the world's religious ideas. He explained that many religions teach love of man, but that Hinduism is the only one to teach such love of animals. Therefore, many devout Hindus never eat meat. Killing an animal for meat is wrong, they feel, for the animal has as much right to live as a man.

Three Ways to Worship

Many thoughtful members of the Hindu faith do not believe that all the worship of the common people is effective. They are as critical as many travelers to India, who say that some of the religious practices are absurd and unintelligent. These thoughtful Hindus regard some of the popular religious practices as sheer superstition. They believe that there are three ways to live a good life. One is the way of good deeds. One is the very important way of knowledge about reality. The third is the way of complete devotion.

Good deeds can be performed by everyone. The poorest member of the lowest caste can do as many good deeds as the well-kept priest in the richest temple in the land. To Hindus, part of doing good deeds is to perform your duty to the best of your ability. There is a place for everyone in this life, and the place that is yours can be filled only by you. Fill it well—and on your way through this world stop often to help the people and animals.

The only happiness deserving the name comes from knowledge of reality—the supreme goal of every Hindu. To this end, men leave their families and go to the forest to study and meditate. Some give up all earthly ties—even to having a funeral service for themselves—to wander about the countryside seeking truth. Some men study Yoga, a system of training for meditation. These men practice breathing and posture exercises untiringly (much more diligently than our football, basketball, or track stars in training). When they have gained the ability to be totally unaware of themselves as persons, they are ready to know the *Atman*.

The easiest way to live the good life is to love all living things and to love the gods. Living the life of unselfish love, one becomes completely devoted to the gods. "Love of men leads to love of God," Hindus say. Some try to intensify their love by looking upon a chosen god in each of these successive roles: parent, master, friend, child, mate, or sweetheart. If such devotional activity brings the worshiper nearer his own true nature, it brings him nearer *Brahman*. There are some Hindus who feel that during their lives they attain the maturity to worship *Brahman* directly. But usually the worship of love is exercised on one of the personal gods.

Ramakrishna

One of the most interesting Hindus of recent times was the man called Ramakrishna. He worshiped after the manner of all three paths. Of himself he declared, "He who was Rama and Krishna is now Ramakrishna." He is considered an incarnation of the supreme lord Vishnu, along with these other two very popular divine descents. When he was just a young man, Ramakrishna was admonished by his brother for not studying more diligently in order to earn his living as a priest. Ramakrishna replied: "And what shall I do with a mere bread-winning education? I would rather acquire that wisdom which will illumine my heart and give me satisfaction forever."

When he was established in a temple supported by a sympathetic, rich widow, Ramakrishna proceeded to live the most devoted kind of life he knew. He became a devotee of Kali, the Divine Mother, represented in Hindu folklore as the wife of the god Shiva. He went beyond all the usual rituals and ceremonials, to make of his life a constant and intense expression of his religious ardor.

He began to think it important to reach the religious goals that all the sects of Hinduism looked upon as important. He worshiped through the methods of Yoga exercises of self-control, through finding the deepest meanings in pleasure, through renunciation of all material and pleasing things, and through intense and blissful love of Krishna. He took up each method in turn and kept practicing it until he had successfully achieved union of *Atman* with *Brahman*.

When this was over, his zeal carried him on to attempts to reap the spiritual values of other religions. He became in turn a Buddhist, a Moslem, and a Christian. From that experience, he became convinced that the goal of all religions was the same. An order of monks named after Ramakrishna is active in India and in other parts of the world, including the United States. He is remembered for his belief in the unity of all religions and for his stress on the importance of the spiritual search.

A Hindu Who Worshiped through Good Deeds

Recently the eyes of Hindus have turned increasingly toward the outer world. India has begun to assert its rightful place as an important nation. This movement was helped a great deal by the efforts and the life of one very devoted Hindu, Gandhi. Before his assassination in 1948, a large part of the world had begun to look to Mahatma Gandhi for guidance in applying religious principles to political situations. For much of his life, he had been engaged in a struggle to better the conditions of the Indian people.

He gained much for the nation through fasting, prayer, and conference, rather than through propaganda, terrorism, and armed rebellion. When his death came, it was at the hands of a radical Hindu, who could not bear Gandhi's insistence that violence not be used against the Moslems living in India.

It was a religious motivation that made his life a compelling example to millions of his fellow Hindus and the center of attention for masses of people all over the world. Gandhi felt that for him the best kind of life was the life of good deeds. When he was thirty-four years old, he undertook the vows of purity and poverty. He dedicated himself to the service of his fellow men. Henceforth no work was too lowly for him to do. Although he had been a member of the merchant caste, he left all caste distinctions behind.

This saintly statesman had a dream toward which he tried to help the world move. The ideal world, he thought, would be achieved by peaceful means, not by war. All religions and all communities and all peoples would have equal privileges. Gandhi insisted on truth and non-violence in every sphere of life. In his insistence, he focused the white light of truth on the inequalities of the caste system and upon untouchability, which he considered to be a blight upon the face of modern India.

He came to feel that the Indian people were being deprived of their rights to their unique culture, and so he initiated the movement which finally led to independence from British rule. The changes he effected were made through the medium of his ascetic habits: his fasts and penances and his renunciation of material comforts. He indeed ceased to live for himself and lived for truth and non-violence.

Gandhi raised so effective a voice for his people that probably some of his writings will someday be included among India's sacred literature. He is already being described by his followers as a savior of his people—an avatar. Of himself, he said simply, "I am a man of peace."

The Influence of Hinduism

For a time we have been looking at the Hinduism that people can see: the gods and goddesses, the images and idols, the temples and sacred places, the rituals and the offerings. We have paused to look at Ramakrishna and Gandhi, two spiritual giants who helped to turn the attention of others to the necessity of living religiously. Thereby the two bettered their religion and their country. Wherever a religion makes a real difference in the lives of people, it becomes a truly magnificent force. Hinduism is such a force. One of the oldest religions in the world—some say the oldest—Hinduism has for centuries helped people to find answers to their deepest questions.

What am I really? In your inner self, replies the Hindu, you are part of God.

What is my life? The Hindu answers that it is a search of whatever length necessary to find God in yourself.

How can I be happy? Only by coming to know God, replies the Hindu.

How can I know God? "He who knows himself will know God."

Which way of worship is best? Hindus have said: "Cattle are of different colors, but all milk is alike; . . . systems of faith are different, but God is one."

Section Two

BUDDHISM

6. The Buddha Asks and Answers

IN THE MIDDLE of the sixth century B.C., many people in India had begun to use some of the religious short cuts described in the preceding chapter about Hindu worship. In general, this was a period of disillusionment. Probably because the people had become thoroughly disillusioned about life, they looked upon reincarnation with increasing dread. Some of them even forgot what their most serious questions were, in their frantic effort to save themselves from the 100,000 lives which they felt they were doomed to live. The art of that time shows people adoring cows, deer, horses, hogs, monkeys, and elephants. Others inflicted tortures on themselves—maintaining one position for a long time, gazing at the brilliant Indian sun, or inhaling smoke and fire.

Many of the priests were not particularly helpful. They, too, had become preoccupied with short cuts in religious living. They were not taking their priestly vocations seriously enough. In one picture from this period, some dogs, intended to symbolize priests, are shown in a grand procession. They are reciting the prayer: "Om, let us eat! Om, bring us food! Lord of food, bring hither food, bring it!" (Om is their shortest word by which God might be addressed.) The people further expressed their low opinion of the priests in this Indian proverb: "Vishnu gets the barren prayers, while the priest devours the offering."

Hinduism was later to regain a place of respected leadership in India; but, during the period described, many people were not able to find in it satisfying answers to life's disturbing problems. Because of this dissatisfaction, some religious reforms shortly arose in an attempt to rid Hinduism of its superficiality. One of these reforms was to be the beginning of Buddhism.

Prince Gautama

At this time when thoughtful men were questioning the value of their native religion, there was born a prince named Gautama. He was the only son of a rich Hindu raja of the warrior caste, and his parents expected him to become a ruler. His father was afraid that Gautama might do what many members of the upper castes did—become a religious seeker or a pilgrim renouncing life. So in his great ambition that his son might follow his own footsteps, the father did everything possible to protect Gautama from influences that would lead him away from this royal life.

Because of the many legends about his early life, it is difficult to know the truth about Gautama. But it seems fairly clear that he was an intelligent and sincere young man, sensitive to all that went on around him. Possibly because of that sensitivity, his father tried to protect him from knowing about the evil and unhappiness that existed outside the palace walls. The stories tell us that Gautama's parents surrounded him with luxuries and all material delights. They attempted to make him feel that all life was happiness and pleasure—that there was no reason to be sad or even very serious. They hoped that Gautama would simply accept the royal life and never question its differences from the lives of other people.

Like all young people, however, Gautama had to live his life in his own way, in spite of his parents' planning. While out driving through a park—so the story goes—he saw four things that made a lasting impression on him. They were more startling than any previous experiences he had had.

First, he noticed a trembling old man, broken-toothed, gray-haired, crooked and bent of body, leaning on a staff. For the first time, he realized that old age must come to everyone. Later, Gautama saw a diseased man, quite loathsome to look upon. Gautama became further dismayed, wondering whether everyone has to suffer, sooner or later. The third disturbing sight was a corpse lying by the side of the road. Apparently for the first time, death became real to the young prince. After these sights had caused him to reflect sadly on the impermanence of life and beauty, he chanced to see a monk, decently clad and of serene countenance. It was then that the thought of retiring from the palace life became very real to Gautama.

The legends tell how his father tried to divert the prince from such serious reflection. Lovely dancing maidens were sent into his palace to entertain him with dance and song. In trying to drive away his sober thoughts, they danced until they collapsed in exhaustion. When Gautama noticed the great alterations in their appearance as they lay in the awkward positions in which they had fallen, he was once more struck with the sadness and ugliness of life. He resolved to leave his comfortable palace immediately. In spite of his baby son and his loyal wife, and in spite of the close watch of his father's palace guards, Gautama took his leave and sought out the solitude of the forest. He was not to return until many years had passed and until many changes had come in his life.

Gautama's Search

Gautama had left the palace with his mind filled with questions: What is life? Why is there unhappiness? In the quiet and timeless Indian forests, he looked for the wise men who could help him find the answers. He hoped to find the contentment he had seen on the face of the monk that day in the park. Since the monk had seemingly found it in the religious life, Gautama determined to look to religion also.

For several years he studied with the best teachers he could find. A very apt pupil, he soon had learned as much as his teachers knew. One of the teachers, impressed with Gautama's learning, invited him to stay and become a partner with him in teaching others. But Gautama felt he could not teach others when he had not yet found the answers he himself was seeking. He knew the scriptures well, but he had not found contentment there. He knew the Yoga exercises, but he had not found full contentment there.

Still the burning questions lingered with him: Why was there unhappiness? How could a man be happy?

He turned more diligently to ascetic practices. He had already left all material pleasure behind. He forced himself to eat less and less, and to meditate more and more. Finally, the legends say, he was living on one grain of rice a day, and he was spending all his time in meditation and study. After six years of persevering search and strenuous self-denial, he was at the point of death. And still he had not found the answers he sought. One day he collapsed from near-starvation.

This proved to be a climax of Gautama's life, for he saw once and for all the futility of what he had been doing. If he continued in his asceticism, he would simply die without finding the answers. What he had been doing, he decided, was as foolish as trying to tie the air into knots. He must go directly to the problem.

Several friends had followed Gautama admiringly because of his religious zeal, but when he resolved to eat again they left him. He was now alone with his thoughts. He sat down under a tree and began to ponder the problem of unhappiness and suffering. So agitated was he, after spending six years in seeking a solution, that he determined to find the answer in thought and meditation before getting up again.

Gautama Becomes the Buddha

After a day and part of a night, he had found his answer. He had become enlightened with the new knowledge. He had become the Buddha, the "awakened one." In the joy of his new understanding, he spoke aloud, though there was no one to hear. No longer, he said, was he going to be subject to the unhappiness of the present life or of repeated births in the round of existence. For he had won insight into man's suffering—its nature, its cause, and its cessation. He was free from the endless round of anxiety and suffering, free from the sense of sorrow and alienation—free to live.

Gautama the Buddha then wondered what he should do next. Should he try to teach others what he had found out for himself after years of seeking? Would anyone else understand him? He soon decided that the good news which was now his could be shared with equally earnest seekers. So he set off for Benares, where he knew he would find five of his former associates who had left him when he decided to take food.

They were the first to hear what he had discovered. His talk to them is usually known as the Sermon on the Turning of the Wheel of the Law. It dealt with the problem of suffering and how to overcome suffering. The points the

Buddha emphasized in this first sermon, in the excited joy of his awakening, have formed the basic ideas of Buddhism. Buddhism means the religion of those seeking to be awakened.

The Middle Path

The path that Gautama had found was one he was to describe as the "Middle Path" between extremes. The extremes to be avoided were the life of sensual indulgence on the one hand and the life of drastic asceticism on the other. Both led to out-of-balance living. Neither led to the true goal of release from suffering. Many people never realize what over-indulgence in comfort and in sensual pleasures have done to their real questions and their real aims. Some who have discovered the evils of over-indulgence come to regard as wicked anything that gives a sense of pleasure. Both groups are reacting too strongly to the human appetites.

Gautama discovered that neither extreme was wise, for neither brings happiness. Over-indulgence has the same final effect on a person as has the release of all tension on the strings of a violin. Extreme self-denial, on the other hand, has the same general effect as tightening the strings on a violin until they are at the breaking point. In neither case is there the right attunement. Harmony is lacking because there is either too little tension or too much. It was this lack of attunement or harmony that Gautama considered to be man's suffering. It was to help men find harmony within themselves and with the universe that he began to teach.

Before the time of Gautama, the Hindu philosophers had taught that the way to self-knowledge was as narrow as the edge of a razor. Gautama discovered the meaning of this for himself and then thought of a more specific way to teach it to others. In all his teachings, however, he never left his Hindu tradition very far behind. Some people and some books give the impression that Gautama tried to start a new religion, or that he disagreed entirely with the other religious teachers of his day. This is not the case.

Gautama simply entered the religious search with a different question: What causes so many people to be unhappy? He took the question to the best teachers he could find, and he could not solve the problem with what they taught him. So he lost respect for the philosophers who wanted only to talk about release from suffering. Gautama liked to remind them that they were playing around with words. He warned his friends against the many schools of philosophy, because the teachers tended to take their own words too seriously.

To find the Middle Way to harmonious living, the Buddha declared, each person must search thoughtfully—not spend his time in wordy arguments. Each person must explore and experiment. *"Happiness he who seeks may win, if he practice the seeking,"* said the Buddha.

7. Why Am I Unhappy?

Even infants suffer. When they are uncomfortable, they cry. As they grow older, they find other ways of expressing their discomfort. But there is no problem of suffering for an infant, since the infant does not really think about it. He simply reacts. Suffering becomes a problem only when people find themselves asking, "Why do I suffer?" Or, as we most often state it, "Why am I unhappy?"

Usually by the time we are ten years of age or a little older, there have been at least a few occasions when we have suffered and have also wondered, "Why this suffering?" Apparently, this question did not occur seriously to Gautama until he was about thirty years of age. This was probably because his parents tried to prevent his experiencing any unpleasantness.

Young people who have grown up in an environment of such over-protection often do not know what it is to face real unhappiness. Personalities of people are different, and the particular rate at which we move from childhood into adolescence varies from one person to another. But, sooner or later, each person has to face the question of the reason for suffering—his own and that of others.

Gautama's whole contribution to the knowledge of mankind centers around the problem of pain or unhappiness. The new knowledge to which he became awakened that night under the tree was about the reason for suffering and how it could be overcome. He first spoke of that knowledge in his sermon to his former colleagues who had left him to go to Benares. The things he mentioned then have become the cardinal principles of Buddhism, even in this day, and they are called the Four Noble Truths. The first truth which he tried to state to his friends was the fact of suffering.

Birth is suffering; decay is suffering; illness is suffering; death, . . . presence of objects we hate, . . . separation from objects we love, . . . not to obtain what we desire is suffering. . . . Clinging to existence is suffering.

When this list is studied, it becomes clear that Guatama was talking about everybody's experience, not just his own. Birth is uncomfortable, both to the mother and to the child, although the child does not consciously remember it. The birth of a new idea, of a new "self" or personality, can also be quite painful; for old habits and old ideas are difficult to discard. Decay also is painful, whether it is decay of a tooth or decay of one's morale and confidence. Illness is uncomfortable, both mentally and physically. Both death and the fear of death, for ourselves and for others, constitute suffering. Either the presence of objects we hate or the absence of objects we love is a painful experience. Not obtaining what we have set our hearts on can make us very miserable. And, as we grow keener in our understanding of life, we become aware that *clinging* to anything can cause us to suffer.

It is unfortunate that so many people have said that the Buddha was pessimistic about life, or that he said that all of life was suffering. If we interpret accurately his words as reported in the records, that is not what he said. He did teach that everything holds the *possibility* of suffering; every phase of life can result in disharmony for a person. The Buddha did not say that all of life *is* suffering.

It is clear that Gautama's interpretation of suffering goes beyond mere physical pain. His strongest emphasis was on suffering of the mind and the emotions. This was the deepest unhappiness. Gautama believed that this suffering was felt by a man who was out of harmony with life. "If I am unhappy, it is because I am not living harmoniously. If I am not living harmoniously, it is because I have not learned to accept the world as it is. Perhaps I am expecting from the world things that I have no right to expect. Perhaps I am clinging too strongly to one part of my world, thus losing touch with the total picture."

Gautama tried to take as his starting point an actual fact of experience, which no one could question and which each one could see for himself. In all human experience, he said, unless there is real understanding, there is an element of pain. He issued the invitation: "Look and see for yourself if this is not true of your life." He asked each person to see that he was not alone in his predicament. All people, sometime in their lives, must face this universal fact—their disharmony. It is not just "my unhappiness"; it is a problem that all men have. Gautama was reminding his friends that "my sorrow" is "world sorrow"—and that the sorrow of the world is "mine."

The Second Noble Truth

Gautama said to his disciples, "I teach only two things, suffering and release from suffering." He was like the doctor who comes to see the sick person. First he learns how the patient is feeling. Then he tries to diagnose the cause of the illness. Gautama, like a good physician, proceeded to the Second Noble Truth, the cause of suffering.

> Now this is the Noble Truth as to origin of suffering. It is the craving thirst that causes the renewal of becomings. This craving thirst is accompanied by sensual delights and seeks satisfaction, now here, now there. It takes the form of craving for the gratification of the senses, or the craving for prosperity.

Suffering is the result of a wrong attitude toward the world and our experiences in it. The world is not bad, but our attitude of craving is what makes it seem bad. This craving, or excessive desire, makes us slaves of whatever we crave. Everyone has seen this principie in operation—a craving for food, a craving for popularity, a craving for success. All make us lose our freedom to choose wisely. What Gautama the Buddha wanted people to see is that he who craves cannot be free and thus cannot be really happy.

You may say that there is a kind of happiness to be found in fulfilling all desires. "If I could just have everything I want and do everything I want to do, I would be so happy." But that kind of happiness boomerangs quickly, for it does not give the deeper contentment that is man's real goal. Often we find people depending more and more on such artificial joys because they are actually afraid to face the deep unhappiness and unrest within themselves.

Gautama advised each person to find for himself the difference between the two kinds of happiness. And he told of his own observations.

When in following after happiness I have perceived that bad qualities developed and good qualities were diminished, then that kind of happiness is to be avoided. And when following after happiness I have perceived that bad qualities were diminished and good qualities developed, then such happiness is to be followed.

He gave some further advice to people who were searching for happiness. The craving which leads to unhappiness, he said, is caused by our ignoring our real needs. If we did not so ignore them, we would not make ourselves unhappy by pursuing things that will never bring satisfaction. This brings us back to the same question that had been raised centuries before by the Hindu wise men: "Who am I really?" Gautama agreed with them that a person is more than the sum of his feelings and thoughts. A person who is wise will always say of any feeling, "This is not the real Me." The Buddha taught that worth-while activity in life should lead to more knowledge of what is the real self, for this brings happiness.

The things people desire frequently do not satisfy their real needs. One Buddhist story tells how Gautama, on one of his journeys, chanced to meet thirty running men. He stopped to ask what the trouble was, and they told their story. While they had been picnicking, one of their woman companions had sneaked away with the belongings of the others, and the men were in hot pursuit of the thief.

The Buddha asked one question: "Which do you think is better—to go on chasing this woman or to go tracking the self?" The men decided that searching for the real self was more important than running after belongings. So, the story says, they became followers of Gautama.

Like the thirty young men, we may be wasting our energies in a fruitless search. If we are wise, we stop to ask ourselves, "What is really worth looking for?" Gautama's answer is quite direct: We should look for the cause of our cravings, and then we should seek to remove the cause.

Suffering ceases with the complete cessation of craving.

A person does not have to remain a slave to his cravings, said Gautama. He can do something about his unhappiness. Each person has a choice about the way he lives. He can fill his life with simple, unquestioned, habitual activities, which have arisen because of cravings. Or he can choose his reactions on the basis of each situation he meets. In the first case, the person is acting out of superficial "needs," in ignorance of his own real needs. In the second case, the person is making possible the realization of his true potentialities. The choice is up to the individual, and it is he who will reap the results.

For example, a person may once find that by eating something he likes he can take his mind off his troubles. Later on, he may choose to eat something good every time he feels unhappy. But this kind of behavior can hardly solve the problem. Actually, he will be simply adding to his troubles while he ignores them, because he may develop indigestion and excess weight and be filled to the brim with problems that are never solved. This is the kind of situation that Gautama had in mind when he spoke of "the craving thirst that causes the renewal of becomings," in his Second Noble Truth. By avoiding an actual grappling with the heart of every difficulty, a person causes himself to have one new problem after another. He builds the new problem on the foundation of all his unsolved problems. By doing so, he continually renews his unhappiness.

When the person meets a new difficulty in the same ineffective way he met old difficulties, he creates new ineffective actions and unwholesome habits. Can this possibly lead to lasting happiness? No, answered the Buddha. Such actions and habits, he further said, come from unexamined and uncontrolled desires. They lead to increasing unhappiness. They keep appearing in a person's life over and over again, in new ways, and even in new lives, according to Buddhist teaching.

Buddhists, like Hindus, believe in transmigration. The ineffective actions and unwholesome habits must be lived out or overcome before one is freed from the endless round of lives that constitute a major part of man's suffering. This is partly what Gautama meant by "clinging to existence" in his First Noble Truth. The whole scheme of transmigration and all unhappiness can be made to cease for a person if he ceases his uncontrolled craving.

Covetousness, resentment, infatuation—these are earmarks of craving. Actions arising from them lead to unhappiness. Happiness is gained by ceasing to crave. The kind of character a person builds today determines the happiness he will have tomorrow. The Buddhist would add that the kind of life one lives today determines in part his chances for happiness in his next reincarnation. Buddhists do not speak of a "person" or "soul"—not even the Hindu Atman—as passing over to another life. It is the influence of past lives that transmigrates to the next life. When a child grows to adulthood, we know that influences from his childhood determine in large measure the kind of adult he will be. And the Buddhists would add that what holds true of one life is true of all conceivable lives, since this earthly life is but one episode among many others.

One may find it difficult to understand the Buddhist theory of past influences and transmigration when extended to many lives. Yet it is easy to see that such a theory contributes to our understanding of our own lives now. What we are today is determined by everything that has entered into our past, including the history of the human race. What we shall be tomorrow is being determined today by the choices we make. We make the best choice, says the Buddhist, when we choose thoughtfully, overcoming selfish and over-strong desires.

8. How Can I Find Happiness?

IF GAUTAMA had said only, "Cease the desires that lead to unhappiness," he would have left his followers without any real help. Fortunately, he did not stop his teaching with just advice. He realized that most people needed help in learning *how* to stop craving. His first sermon concluded with an important Fourth Noble Truth. In giving this last statement of the truths he had discovered, Gautama described the way a person might stop craving. Since Gautama's time, this way has been called the "Holy Eight-Fold Path." The eight steps are specific ways Gautama suggested for people to release themselves from the clutches of their own desires.

(1) Right Viewpoint

The first step toward happiness, Gautama said, is the *right viewpoint* on unhappiness. Before a person can make any progress, he must look at his problem for what it is. When he sees that it is his ignoring of the true facts of his life that causes his trouble, and when he has accepted his responsibility for that trouble, then he has entered upon the Path. Gautama did not claim to have found an original way to happiness. He described it as being very ancient. But he felt that most people were not aware of it.

Gautama said that so long as we see life from the wrong viewpoint we will go on craving things as though the things would make us happy. This is a way of deceiving ourselves. We must learn to see for ourselves why it is a delusion. Then we are ready to take the second step, which Gautama called *right aspiration*.

(2) Right Aspiration

Everyone aspires after something. The trouble is that most of us, in our confused mental and emotional condition, have aspired after the wrong things. We have not focused our desires and efforts on worth-while objectives. But when we renounce false values that lead us into unhappiness, we are in a position to choose the true values. The Buddha pointed to kindness and love as being true values. Such values can be attained only when a person has gone beyond the point where his primary concern is "I," "me," and "mine." It is after self-centeredness ceases that true kindness and love are shown in a free and spontaneous way.

The Buddha's first two steps in the Path deal with the importance of getting attitudes changed for the better. The next three steps deal with the kind of conduct that ought to flow from right attitudes.

(3) Right Speech

The third step is right speech. A person following the Buddha's Path can no longer take delight in gossip, slander, and abusive or idle talk. His speech will be controlled, considerate, and thoughtful, because it stems from kind attitudes toward others. Some people commit worse crimes through what they say than hardened criminals do. Gautama recognized, just as modern psychologists do, that this is a stumbling block to real maturity.

(4) Right Behavior

The next step in the Buddha's Path is the important step of right behavior. Gautama did not describe fully the scope of this step. But his followers gradually drew up lists of the things one was not supposed to do. One typical list says that a person must not kill, steal, be impure, lie, or drink intoxicants. However, such negative commandments are incidental to the importance of what Gautama said about behavior. He knew that it was much more important to encourage people to do certain things than to order them not to do others.

To Gautama, right behavior meant love. Gautama taught that "all that we are is the result of what we have thought." Therefore, we should not harbor feelings of resentment or hatred. Feelings and thoughts wreck chances for happiness, as truly as do actions. "'He abused me, he beat me, he defeated me, he robbed me'—in those who harbor such thoughts, hatred will never cease," warned Gautama. For he had discovered that "hatred does not cease by hatred at any time; hatred ceases by love." And he said at another time, "Let a man overcome anger by love, let him overcome evil by good."

Gautama frequently told his friends that even if they were attacked violently, either with abusive language or with sticks and stones, they were not to fight back or to dwell on resentful thoughts. "If someone curses you, you must suppress all resentment and make the firm determination, 'My mind shall not be disturbed, and no angry word shall escape my lips. I will remain kind and friendly, and with loving thoughts and no secret spite.' If then you are attacked with fists, with stones, with sticks, with swords, you must suppress all resentment and preserve a loving mind with no secret spite."

(5) Right Livelihood

To a man who was really earnest about finding the true happiness, the fifth step was the next logical one. It is right livelihood. There were certain occupations a man could not engage in without damaging himself and others seriously, Gautama felt. Any business that involved injuring life in any form was not to be followed. This included, for Buddhists, the trade of the butcher, of the vendor of poisons (dopes, drugs, and the like), of the slave trader or the slave owner. One must not engage in making or distributing liquors. Neither must one be a soldier.

This was in sharp contrast to one teaching of the Hindu religion, with which Gautama was so familiar. Hindus felt that a man was born into his rightful occupation. But the Buddha was convinced that one must not hinder others in his own search for the happiest adjustment to life. Hence a person might have to change his occupation. Gautama himself was surrounded by people who had renounced the normal family life and usual occupations to enter the monastic way of life. Ideally, he thought, all sincere religious seekers would do this. In this way, they would most surely find lasting contentment. Yet later an order of Buddhist laymen was established. And more and more Buddhists through the years have continued to live with their families, finding suitable occupations, rather than leaving such things behind for the monastery.

(6) Right Effort

The sixth step is a move beyond the level of conduct. It is right effort, and to the Buddha those words had a special meaning. Right effort means that one must find for himself his own proper rate of speed on the Holy Eight-Fold Path to true happiness. A religious seeker must not move too slowly or too quickly. And there is no happiness to be gained in trying to keep pace with someone else. You are yourself, with your own needs and your own tempo. One task in learning to know our true selves is to learn to travel at our own best pace.

(7) Right Mindfulness

Gautama's seventh emphasis was *right mindfulness*. He declared that it is the mind that leads man into most of his disharmonious living. Physical desires might be distracting, the Buddha admitted, but usually that is because the vivid imagination creates too many desires. The desire to eat in itself does not make one unhappy. Unhappiness develops from excessive eating or excessive desire to eat. Part of right mindfulness meant learning to see physical desires and everything else for what they actually were, not as the imagination had made them appear.

The Buddha's aim was to teach people that objects that appeal to the senses have power to make us unhappy because they may lead to *excessive desires*. He was aware that the average man had a habit of "idealizing" women. He urged his followers to overcome this habit of enslavement to a pretty face. The story is told of a traveler who once asked a Buddhist monk, "Tell me, have you seen a woman walking along this way?" The monk replied, "I cannot say whether it is a woman or a man that passed this way. This I know, that a set of bones is traveling this road." This is Buddhist *right mindfulness* carried to the extreme.

Gautama hoped that his fellow travelers on the Path would develop a calmness in their search for happiness. In that way, each would learn to stand off from himself and observe his own passions as unexcitedly as he might look at the stars in the heavens. Each was to practice considering his emotions for what they were, both externally and internally. This was suggested for both painful and pleasant feelings. The Buddhist monk tries to remember constantly that his feelings are short-lived, coming and going. In this way he is able to hold himself undisturbed by his emotions, not craving anything or clinging to anything. A person who can accept his feelings in this objective way will be less inclined to be swept off his feet by them.

(8) Right Contemplation

The final step in the Path is called *right contemplation*. Gautama had a great appreciation for some of the prevailing Yoga practices of his day. Although he had not found in Yoga the full answers to his questions about unhappiness, he had been helped by such practices to "silence" his mind. Therefore, he told his followers of its values.

The Yoga discipline was taught individually. It involved learning how to quiet the irrelevant thoughts of the mind, until the person could come directly to knowledge of his own true needs. This contemplation that Gautama recommended was not a process of reasoning or logic. It was a different way of knowing—by insight or intuition. Because Gautama recognized that people vary greatly in temperament, he suggested several dozen modes of training the mind for right contemplation. These ways were developed by his followers into the Yoga practices that are still important to many zealous Buddhists.

Nirvana

Gautama emphasized that a serious follower of the Eight-Fold Path would achieve Nirvana. The minimum meaning of Nirvana is the extinction of all craving, resentment, and covetousness. As we have seen, to the Buddha such extinction of craving and other improper attitudes was true happiness. Nirvana has another meaning, which is just as important to most Buddhists. That is the release from all future reincarnations, escape from the "Round of Becoming."

Just as Buddhists do not speak of a soul or the *Atman*, so they hesitate to talk about a Supreme Spirit such as *Brahman*. They feel that such matters cannot be surely determined. Talk, they say, is unimportant. Knowing and searching are important. But whether or not there is a soul or a Supreme Spirit, Buddhists believe there is transmigration. For the influences and habit-tendencies of one life will go on reproducing themselves in one form or another for an indefinite time in the future.

Nirvana is not a place. It is a condition of the mind. Nirvana is reached after earnest thoughtfulness and vigorous effort. Thoughtfulness is one of the chief virtues of Buddhists. Thoughtlessness is deplored. Buddhists have compared a thoughtless man to a monkey feverishly searching for food in a forest.

Nirvana does not mean the loss of personal consciousness that comes with death, for Gautama achieved it and then spent many years trying to help others realize it. However, Buddhists soon found it necessary to talk about ultimate Nirvana. This could be achieved after one had died. They called it *Parinirvana*.

A truly happy person is the one who has given the thought and effort necessary to realize Nirvana. The Buddha did not respect titles or castes—even the highest castes in India. He said that a man did not reach happiness by the status of the family into which he was born. Had not he himself been born a prince and yet been for a time among the unhappiest of the unhappy? Not by birth, not by wealth, does one discover how to overcome suffering. By seeking to overcome unwholesome desires, by keeping to the practical Eight-Fold Path, by self-knowledge—by these one attains lasting happiness.

9. Which Path Shall I Take?

TODAY about one-fifth of the world's people are Buddhists. The story of their religion goes back to the day Gautama sat under the Bo-tree and arose with a new understanding of life. Buddhism began when Gautama's five disciples heard him tell about his experiences. They became his followers again, this time with real conviction. If they had keep the good news to themselves, Buddhism would never have begun. As it was, they gladly told all who would hear. The number of followers of the "Enlightened One" slowly grew.

Gautama spent the rest of his long life teaching and loosely organizing groups of followers. Finally, when he was more than eighty, he died. His saddened followers continued to meet and study and meditate together, held by the memory of his talking and meeting with them. At first they kept very closely to his teachings. They showed the power of his influence by their insistence on doing just what they would have done had he been still with them.

Gradually some of them began to see and show things that reminded them of their master. These things became symbols of Buddhism. The Bo-tree, the "Tree of Wisdom," reminds Buddhists of his enlightenment. The lotus blossom is a reminder that any person can rise up, just as pure, from whatever surroundings. The Buddhist wheel is a reminder of the Buddha's first sermon on eternal truth and the endless Round of Becoming. The monks would turn the wheel as a symbol of putting the law of eternal truth into motion.

Sometime during the early years after his death, Gautama's followers wrote down his sayings and teachings, dividing them into three sections. This scriptural work is known as the *Tripitaka*, which means "three baskets." Other important Buddhist teachers interpreted some of these scriptures. They, too, said things that Buddhists wished to remember. Additions were made to the scriptures.

Gradually, followers of Gautama began to differ in their opinions on what was most important in the search for understanding of life. The early disagreements grew and developed into two great branches. The branch of Buddhism that claims to have changed least from the form of the Buddha's teaching is *Hinayana* or Southern Buddhism. Hinayana Buddhists dwell, for the most part, in Thailand, Ceylon, and Burma. The larger branch is *Mahayana* or Northern Buddhism, which is a dominant religion of China, Japan, Korea, and Tibet.

The two terms have an interesting meaning. Hinayana means "small vehicle" and indicates that a small number of people are able to achieve release from life's sorrow by its rigorous discipline. Mahayana means "great vehicle" and means that a large number of people are able to fulfill its requirements along the path to salvation.

Neither of these branches is a real force in the religious life of India, the mother country of Buddhism. It was a long time after Gautama's life before people came to look upon Buddhism as a religion apart from Hinduism. After missionary monks had begun to carry Buddhist ideas to other lands, the Indian people slowly began to reject it as a separate religion, mostly because its teachings did not include some ideas and practices that had been a part of their traditions and their society for centuries. Since a few of the Buddha's ideas were adopted by some Hindus, the influence of the gentle, thoughtful prince survives in modern India. However, the Buddha's contributions to religious truth live on largely in other lands. And in these other lands of the Far East, much of the full glory of Buddhism has been achieved.

Hinayana Buddhism: The Path of Self-Reliance

In Thailand, Ceylon, and Burma, there are many devoted Buddhists, who believe themselves to be following the way of life taught by the master teacher, Gautama. The underlying basis of their faith is that one is responsible for his own salvation. A person's past, present, future—all are up to him. As the Buddha taught, so they believe. There is no god who can arrange that salvation. No one can do it for you.

The truly devout Hinayana Buddhist is the *arhat*, whose first duty is his own salvation. He works diligently to achieve release from the sorrow of many lives. He loses himself in the search for release by concentrating on the teaching and philosophy that come from the teachings of Gautama. His material needs for food, shelter, and clothing are limited to the very minimum. Even these are usually supplied by other believers, who cannot break all ties in the way the arhat has done. They hope to gain merit through helping him.

As in all other religions, there are few people who can and do put everything else second to the religious search. Recognizing this fact, the monks teach the people who have no other way of learning the truths as the Buddha taught them. There are no priests in Hinayana Buddhist communities, but there is an active order of monks. They teach the people what they consider to be essential: to grow spiritually every day and to show kindness to all things. Present-day Buddhists learn what Gautama taught the lay people who flocked to learn from him. They are expected to observe the first five rules of the ancient order of monks. They are also taught to recite the universal Buddhist statement of the "refuges."

> I take refuge in the Buddha;
> I take refuge in the Doctrine;
> I take refuge in the Order.

The teachings of the monks spread throughout the Hinayana Buddhist lands because almost all the young boys spend time in monasteries as a part of their education. There they take part in study, in religious ceremonies, in meditation, and in all other activities of the monastery. The monks who teach them emphasize the most important idea in Hinayana Buddhism—that they must learn to be responsible for their own religious development. They are encouraged to examine and question religious traditions. They are not to accept a doctrine or a practice that is not helpful in their search for Nirvana. They learn the values of self-control and moderation in all things.

After such an education, some of the boys decide to become ordained and live as monks the rest of their lives. Everyone is pleased at this turn of events, since all believers feel that this is the only way to assure release from the endless and sorrowful cycle of lives. The family, however saddened they may be at what amounts to a loss of their son, comfort themselves with the remembrance that they must not cling overmuch to anything. They know that he is working to attain Nirvana. There are solemn ceremonies to mark monastic vows. The boy dramatizes the Great Renunciation that Gautama made, when he left his family and his kingdom, took up his monk's robe and begging bowl, and set out in search of salvation.

Buddhists believe that the teachings of Gautama still apply to life in the twentieth century, because they came straight from Gautama's grappling with life. Since his wisdom came directly, out of what happened to him and not out of books, present-day Hinayana Buddhists are encouraged to go through the same kind of learning process he did. Most of them decided that their Master was right in his understanding of the nature of sorrow and how to overcome it. Therefore, generation after generation of Buddhists find the age-old teachings valuable. This is the reason that the Hinayana Buddhists of today are still very close to the spirit of the earliest Buddhists in ancient India.

Like most religions, Hinayana Buddhism has been with its people so long that some social customs now seem to be a part of the religion. Even very young children are taught the need of self-control, of the Oriental respect and reverence for parents, neatness of person and home, serenity of emotions and bearing. In some homes and in temples there are idols or statues of the Buddha, beside which the people lay white flowers as a sign of their reverence.

Shot through all the colorful but serene fabric of Hinayana Buddhism are the essential ideas. Man must make himself wise for his own salvation, starting now. He must show sympathy and peace in his dealings with all living beings. He must learn to control all his thoughts and his actions, because these are what make up himself in this life, and these are what influence all succeeding lives.

No act or thought stops upon your completion of it. It continues in what it causes to happen. If you become angry and give a tongue-lashing to a friend, that is not the end of the act and the words. The friend, hurt by your anger, may react in anger at you or even at another. In that way the act continues and lives on in other acts. The same cycle is the way of the kind act also. Your show of kindness toward a person or even an animal causes the receiver of the kindness to act in the same way to a third party.

A man reaps what he sows. Buddhists believe that character is made up of the thoughts and actions that a person has "sown." The effects of the thoughts and actions are what is reborn—not the "inner self" or the soul. A person has only to think of the life lived by Gautama, who taught more by example than by words. He has shown men that all can educate themselves to enlightenment and Nirvana, even if it takes more than one lifetime. The effects of Gautama's good and kind thoughts and actions have continued until today and will for all time, even though Gautama released himself from the wheel of rebirth. Everyone is able to do what Gautama did.

Mahayana Buddhism: The Path of Mutual Aid

In its own way, Mahayana Buddhism is very different from Hinayana Buddhism. This Northern Buddhism dates from the years immediately following the death of Gautama, when his followers were yearning for the old days when he was with them. Always they treated his memory with reverence. Some of them soon came to attach special importance to anything that reminded them of his life. The meeting places of some disciples gradually began to look like temples. Profound changes took place in the interpretations of the scriptures. These newer forms of Buddhism took the name Mahayana. Mayahana arose to meet the spiritual needs of the simple, hard-working, common people.

Mahayana Buddhists believe that they are right in their efforts to get help with their religious growth. They point to the Buddha's own example of unselfish service in teaching others how to find the path to Nirvana, even when he himself had reached the goal. Love such as he had thus shown became the supreme teaching of the different schools and sects of Mahayana Buddhism. Mahayana Buddhists do not idealize the arhat, who "wandered lone as a rhinoceros," looking for Nirvana. Instead, they have a loving respect for a compassionate saint, a Bodhisattva. This is a person who is so attuned to the sufferings and hopes of all human beings that he refuses to enter into Nirvana himself until all others can enter with him. This is the dominant ideal in Chinese and Japanese Buddhism.

The story of Amitabha (or Amida, as he is called in Japan) illustrates the Bodhisattva's place in Mahayana Buddhism. Although Amitabha was originally a Bodhisattva, he is now referred to as a Buddha, since in Mahayana Buddhism there are many Buddhas. Amitabha Buddha is next to Gautama in the hearts of Northern Buddhists. (In northern lands, Gautama is called Sakyamuni Buddha, meaning "the sage of the Sakya clan," to which his family belonged.) According to legends, Amitabha was a monk who lived infinite ages ago. He made a vow that he would devote all of his wisdom and merits to the saving of others. Through the years, he built up what might be called a "Treasury of Merit," a tremendous checking account of goodness. Mahayana Buddhists believe that anyone in need of merit can draw upon this account by meditating upon the compassion of Amitabha and calling upon his name.

In Buddhist writings, the checking account is often referred to as the "Ship of Amitabha's Vow." The "Ship of the Vow" is designed to carry individuals across the floods of life to a "Pure Land" or Western Paradise, which Amitabha established for all those who would have faith in him. Amitabha is the central figure of some schools and sects in Mahayana Buddhism. These groups comprise what is called "Pure Land" Buddhism, because they believe that anyone who has faith in Amitabha will enter into the Western Paradise upon death, and thus escape indefinitely the sorrow of rebirth.

The best known Bodhisattva is Kwan-Yin (Kwannon in Japan), who is a goddess of mercy. Ancient stories tell Mahayana Buddhists that she lived long ago. She was so filled with love and kindness for all mankind that she took a vow to help any persons anywhere who needed her. She would not even enter Paradise upon her death. Instead, she went to live on an island, where there is now a temple to symbolize her presence. Buddhists may pray to her for aid in the task of collecting enough merit to escape transmigration. Some make pilgrimages to the temple on her island in the Eastern Sea of China.

The basic idea in both these stories is mutual helpfulness. Buddhists tell us that these are legends written in picture-language. They are designed to show us that we are not independent. We are part of the interdependence of all of life. The influence of my thoughts and deeds is intertwined with the influence of yours. No one is an island, all by himself in the sea of life. Each person is a part of the mainland. An artist drawing a picture to symbolize our lives would not draw vertical threads stretching up from each of us to some heaven above. He would instead draw a complex net of threads, because each individual contributes to all others. Therefore, Buddhists believe that Amitabha and Kwan-Yin give of their merits to all.

A Buddhist poet has beautifully expressed the idea of what the Bodhisattva is and what he does:

> I would be a protector of the unprotected, a guide to wayfarers, a ship, a dyke, and a bridge for them who seek the further Shore; a lamp for them who need a lamp, a bed for them who need a bed, a slave for all beings who need a slave.
> If I fulfill not my vow by deeds, I shall be false to all beings, and what a fate will be mine. . . . If I labor not this very day, down, down I fall.

Wherever Mahayana Buddhism has attracted large numbers of believers, there are monks, philosophers, and students. There is also an organized religion with many gods, and with temples, priests, and ceremonies. It is still desirable to become a monk if it is possible, but there are many ways for a lay person to take part in his religion. There are rituals of individual worship and chanting services led by the monks. Some sects have sermons and hymn singing in their services. Some have "Sunday schools." In some places, the Young Men's Buddhist Association is a well-known feature. Some large cities in the United States have Buddhist churches where you may see some of these new forms of worship.

Most Mahayana Buddhists stress that Sakyamuni Buddha was not just a man who lived in a certain time and in a certain place. He was much more than that. He was a disclosure of eternal truth. Whenever a person worships the Buddha, he is actually worshiping the eternal Buddha-nature, which Gautama revealed. The world is not so made that this revelation could come only in our age. Mahayana Buddhists believe that there have been other Buddhas in other ages. They look for the coming of Maitreya, the future Buddha in the next age. In all, they speak of untold numbers of Buddhas, who have revealed Truth to men of every age. Present in them was the same Buddha-nature, which can be discovered in everyone. All can achieve enlightenment or Buddhahood. Many say that *Bodhisattvas* are the Buddhas of some future age.

There is another side of Mahayana Buddhism, which is quite different from the ideas we have been examining. It is called Ch'an in China and Zen in Japan. In Japan there is an active church based on its philosophy, but it is primarily a school of thought to which many monks belong. Zen does not stress any of the ideas about saviors, a Western Paradise, faith, or god. Its philosophers say that all ideas and religious practices are like shells which must be broken if the egg is to be eaten. People cling to ideas and practices, forgetting what it is they attempt to explain or show. To cling to ideas is like trying to cling to the wind or capture it in a box. The wind eludes you. So does Truth, if you limit yourself to one thought or one act.

To the Zen Buddhist, teachers, books, or scriptures can be only pointers—like a finger pointing at the moon. Small children always look at the finger which points, rather than at the thing to which it points. Most adults also become much more preoccupied by the pointer than by that to which it points. The mind, the mouth, the eye, the ear, and the hand provide us with opinions, impressions, and actions. But these are only ways of describing or showing what has happened to us. The danger is that we become wrapped up in our opinions and impressions and actions and forget the experience that caused them. It is like putting too much value on a frame, rather than on the picture it was designed to enhance. Or it is like treasuring the cover of a book and forgetting the story in it.

Zen Buddhists say that you find truth only in your experience, not in thinking about it or listening to someone talk about his experience. To understand the meaning of life, one must *live*, not make up theories about it. One day a famous Zen teacher who liked to shock his pupils threw all of the statues of the Buddha into the fire to provide more warmth in the room. This is what Zen says everyone must do with all of his ideas—burn them up so that they will not clutter up one's mind unduly. All theories must be broken like so many clay idols. Zen Buddhists even teach that if a person says the word "Buddha" he should wash out his mouth.

Zen teachers know that by word of mouth they cannot teach the truth that comes only from experience. When young men come asking about Nirvana or the Buddha, Zen teachers often answer with anything that comes into their minds, however absurd. Or they may resort to a sort of "shock therapy" in which they strike the pupils. They hope that such a surprising answer will startle the pupils into understanding. They repeatedly tell their disciples that concentration upon a problem will not bring an answer, because you merely become tangled in your own thinking. You must live a life of moderation and kindness and go about your daily activities, learning to question your impressions and thoughts. Suddenly some day you will understand.

The Outreach of Buddhism

No section of the world is changing more rapidly than the Far East. Conditions in Buddhist lands have changed many times since Gautama first developed his answers to the riddle of why men suffer. Both Mahayana and Hinayana Buddhism have proved adaptable to changing conditions and to different peoples. The world of tomorrow will grow out of the world of today. So Buddhism will probably continue to be a real influence in the lives of our Far Eastern neighbors. Mahayana Buddhism is widening its influence by sending missionaries to new sections, in the belief that what the Buddha discovered can help almost everyone.

"Why am I unhappy?" The Buddha suggests: Because you fill yourself with *wanting*, until the wanting is a thirst that cannot be satisfied even by the things you want.

"How can I be happy?" By ceasing to want. Just as a fire dies down when no fuel is added, so your unhappiness will end when the fuel of excessive desire is taken away. When you conquer selfish, unwise habits and hopes, your real happiness will emerge.

Section Three

CHINESE RELIGIONS

10. Taoism: The Way of Naturalness and Noncoercion

For as long as we can remember, the news about China has been news about changes in the way of life of the people. Civil wars, international wars, revolutions, new political developments. Always changes such as these take their toll in the whole life of all the people affected. In China, as elsewhere, religions have been forced to change. Many of the old traditions and ceremonies and ideas are no longer respected or observed or understood by today's Chinese.

The ancient country of China was relatively untouched by modern scientific and educational advancements until the beginning of the twentieth century. Yet, centuries ago, there lived a Chinese sage named Lao-tse, who believed and taught that the world moved according to a divine pattern, which is reflected in the rhythmic and orderly movements of nature. The sum of wisdom and of happiness for man, said Lao-tse, is that he adjust himself to this order and himself reflect the way the world moves.

Lao-tse's life and thought have added depth to Chinese life and thought. The world would be the poorer without him. His teachings, together with those of later followers who believed as he did, make up the thoughtful basis of Taoism. Yet, when we look back carefully into the past of China—to about 600 b.c.—we see only a faint, shadowy outline of this sage, humorist, philosopher, and prophet. The figure of Lao-tse comes close to being legendary. However, many scholars claim that such a person did live. Stories tell us that he was visited by Confucius and that the two philosophers conversed together. Lao-tse is mentioned in books written in the generation just after his own. According to tradition, Lao-tse himself is supposed to have written the *Tao-Teh-King*, the fascinating little book on which much of Taoism is based.

Lao-tse was first moved to speak because he saw around

him many people who were perplexed by unanswered questions about their lives. The questions were not very different from the ones you and I ask even today. Like all basic human questions, they have been repeated by generations. "What am I? What is my life? Am I living the best life I can? What could I be? How can I do better? What are the results of trying to do better?"

The Chinese looked upon their world in an optimistic way, and when they asked, they asked hopefully and confidently. The world, they observed, was a good place for a man. It could be depended upon. All their experience in daily contacts with the world had shown them that it was orderly and dependable. Nature did not operate by whim. The Chinese seemed to sense that they "belonged" to nature.

Yet Lao-tse looked at the people around him and saw some of them struggling for happiness without remembering what their traditions taught them. He saw people trying to change what life offered, instead of accepting it. And he said: "You seek wisdom, goodness, and contentment. In the ways you are trying to attain them, you are blind and foolish. Can you not see that wisdom is trust, goodness is acceptance, and contentment is simplicity? This is the way of the world."

The Way of the World

In days earlier even than Lao-tse's, the way of the world had been given a name, the Tao (pronounced dow), which means simply "way" or "way to go." It has been translated as "nature" or "the way of nature." It is the way the universe moves and has its being. Man is a part of the universe. When men are most natural, they move according to the laws of interdependence and interaction of all parts of the world. If Tao were allowed freely to operate within men, then everything would be at its best, for the Tao is the way of perfection: perfect balance, perfect harmony. It is the way—there is no other.

The Tao is the source of all created things. It is responsible for bringing all things into existence, even the Chinese gods. The Tao itself has never been considered as a god. The Tao is reality. It existed before there was any universe. It created all existence and continues to keep it in operation through the release of its energy. Rise and fall, flow and ebb, existence and decay—through such an alternation of the *Tao's* energy, existence began and will continue. Even so, the *Tao* never forces a person to act in a certain way. The *Tao* simply operates. That is all.

Taoism was so named because Lao-tse and his followers were insistent upon the *Tao* as the way of life. "Getting back to nature" was their goal—"nature" being understood to mean the natural and proper way of all things. So completely did the early Taoists follow this line of belief that they went about China calling for the end of human ceremonies and customs and even civilization itself, because these were the result of interfering with nature.

The Way of Men

The early Taoists frequently referred to a past "Golden Age," when men had lived in peace and harmony because they were natural, free from artificiality, simple—in short, men of *Tao*. The good things that all men seek had been lost when that age had passed. Men would find them only when they returned to the simplicity and utter naturalness that had characterized the Golden Age.

"Nature" is the key to all the Taoists' answers to the questions life makes us ask. A person's highest good and his sincere happiness are to be found through conforming with the way of all nature, the *Tao*. When one is natural, he is relaxed within and able to accept what life offers. When one is ambitious or aggressive, he contradicts his true nature. In the ensuing civil war within himself, he strikes his possible happiness a fatal blow.

While Lao-tse was calmly suggesting that men must relax and accept the world as it is, instead of trying to change it, there were many others who loudly voiced their disagreement. Reformers and philosophers, Confucius among them, walked the land, telling all who would listen that the only way to regain happiness and prosperity was for all people to become virtuous. When every person learned to do his duty and to fulfill all of his responsibilities, then the land and all its people would be blessed. They, too, spoke of a past golden age, when happiness was the rule rather than the exception. But, they said, its values could be realized again when the people learned how to behave toward each other.

"Not so, not so!" cried the early Taoists. Virtue, duty—

these are achieved by those who let themselves go and do what comes naturally. Why should a man strive for goodness? Goodness comes of itself when all rules are forgotten and effort ceases. Virtue is never gained by seeking it. Duty is performed only when you are not trying to perform it.

Lao-tse had little sympathy for the typical reformer who wished to add rule after rule for proper living. It is after people have lost their way, said he, that the reformer cries, "Be good, be righteous! I will tell you how." When a family is no longer getting along very well, the parents start telling the children to be respectful and obedient. This applies to nations, too, for only in times of national confusion are people anxious about patriotism.

Nature never argues the way persons do. Nature just goes on being natural. And what argument can change the way of the world? Gravity does not debate with us or insist; it just operates. In such ways, nature shows us the Tao. Lao-tse pointed out that the Tao is never forceful, yet there is nothing that it does not accomplish. Precisely because of its unceasing, unstriving, uncoercing operation, the Tao is the only power.

The man who lives by Tao will not use force, for force defeats his higher aims. The man who tries to shape the world into what he wants it to be damages himself and others in the attempt. He who insists or strives for something gets involved in his own efforts and merely loses the value of the thing he seeks. Thus he damages his ideal, defeats his purpose, and fails miserably.

Men should learn from a pond of muddy water. No amount of stirring can clear it. But when it is left alone, it becomes clear by itself. So it is with men and with nations. Rulers particularly must understand this. Lao-tse once said that one should govern people as he would cook a small fish—gently. Too much cooking, too much handling make it fall to pieces or destroy its flavor. As for the people who presume to teach others, they must also grasp this idea. He who thinks he knows a lot about others may think he is wise. But only he who knows himself has hold upon the true and the important.

The Man of Tao

Lao-tse and Chuang-tse, the best-known later Taoist (around 350-275 B.C.), must have spoken reluctantly, for the real Tao is not the Tao that can be expressed in words.

It is impossible to describe literally the man of Tao. Yet these two men were pressed for definitions. And so Lao-tse drew a word picture:

> He is cautious, like one who crosses a stream in winter;
> He is hesitating, like one who fears his neighbors;
> He is modest, like one who is a guest;
> He is yielding, like ice that is going to melt.

Taoists feel that such descriptions of the poised and serene person are true, not because Lao-tse or anyone else has said them—but because they reflect the nature of things, the Tao.

Chuang-tse was fishing one day when some high officials of the government of his province came to visit him. As he continued to fish, they flattered him by speaking of his wisdom and offered him a high governmental post, which would bring him recognition and respect from many people. Without interrupting his fishing, Chuang-tse asked the gentlemen if they knew of the sacred tortoise, dead over three thousand years, which the prince kept safely enclosed in a chest on the altar of his ancestors. Then he asked them, "Do you think this tortoise would rather be dead and have its remains revered, or be alive and wagging its tail in the mud of its pond?"

"It would rather be alive," they replied, "wagging its tail in the mud."

"You may be on your way," said Chuang-tse. "I too prefer to wag my tail in the mud in my own pond."

What Is Worth-while? The Three Treasures

Then what is of value? And for what should a person spend his efforts? A person cannot simply sit and fold his hands and wait. Since he lives in a group of people, he has to think of others. The early Taoists faced the problem of living in an everyday world. They knew that they must live their philosophy, as well as think it. They decided that there were three things—three treasures, they called them —that are the supreme guides of the man to Tao. These three are love, moderation, and humility. How do these three qualities help the man of Tao to live in the world? "Being loving, one can be brave; being moderate, one can be ample; not venturing to go ahead of the world, one can be the chief of all officials."

One who sees the Tao within himself sees the Tao in others and in all the world. It is this person who sees that his true welfare is good for all men. The good for all men is his good, too. This is what Lao-tse meant by being loving. The man of Tao will act with goodness toward all men, to the so-called good people as well as to the so-called bad, even returning love for great hatred. If this is not done, regardless of how justly one deals with the hatred, some of the hatred or its results will remain. "Being loving, one can be brave." The man of Tao trusts the world, and the world can be entrusted to him.

In all his thoughts and actions, the man of Tao is moderate. Excesses in any direction are blocks to contentment. The man of Tao would not decide in advance exactly what course of action he would take in a given situation. Neither would he decide in advance that he would not conduct himself in a certain way. He would remember always that whatever presents itself as the simplest and most natural way to act or to think is the way to follow. In this way, his actions are always sufficient and always right. "Being moderate, one can be ample."

Lao-tse and his followers never sought high places in governmental offices, for this was against their convictions. One cannot help people by trying to direct their actions. And they pointed out how one could better achieve his purposes by holding himself in a humble place. In our world there is no place for some to be ahead of others. There is room only for all to live naturally and in mutually helpful ways. Let no one seek private gain or personal success.

Heaven is eternal, the Earth everlasting.
How come they to be so? It is because they do not foster
    their own lives;
That is why they live so long.
Therefore the Sage
Puts himself in the background; but is always to the fore.
Remains outside; but is always there.
Is it not just because he does not strive for any personal
    end
That all his personal ends are fulfilled?

These qualities are treasures that do not lie buried somewhere so deeply that a teacher or friend or philosopher is needed to dig them out for us. They are found when we become aware of those things which we ordinarily ignore in our deepest nature. Simply by peeling back through the layers of our fears and habits and superficial aspirations, we find such treasures. A lack of these qualities shows us a person who is forced, unnatural, and unhappy.

What Must I Do?

Duty is to be performed, not because a man feels obligated to do it, but more because he does not feel that he must not do it. The man of Tao would conform to the world to the extent required to cause him least difficulty in living in harmony with the Tao. It is clear that he could not live harmoniously if he were constantly plotting to get out of responsibility and to overthrow governments and institutions. It is clear also that he would not live harmoniously if he were constantly planning to take over larger shares of responsibility and to reform or strengthen the things about him. The world is like a broth that too many cooks are about to spoil. The wise man will refuse to add any ingredients, nor will he stir. He prefers to wait for a proper and natural blend.

But how can we just sit back and let things happen without doing anything to help or hinder? It is difficult to do, but it is simple. It is as simple and as difficult as relaxing. Chuang-tse gave this advice:

> A man feels a pleasurable sensation before he smiles, and smiles before he thinks how he ought to smile. Resign yourself to the proper sequence of things.

The world is not ours to take by the horns and steer. The world is ours to live in and to understand. Harmony is not born of aggressive notes, striking out on their own. It is born of humble notes, yielding confidently and quietly in accord.

Chuang-tse once told a story about a man who struck out on his own, instead of yielding in confidence to the Tao. This man was so afraid of his shadow and he so disliked his own footsteps that he determined to get away from them. However, the more he moved, the more footsteps he made. And despite his fast running, he never left his shadow far behind. So he decided that he was going too slowly. He ran his fastest, without pausing for rest. As a result, he weakened and finally died. He did not know that he could have lost his shadow in the shade and put an end to his footsteps by keeping still. Foolish indeed was he. Woe to the reformers and the moralists who come preaching of purity and goodness, says Chuang-tse—they run from their own shadows.

What Is Right? What Is True?

When one really stops to analyze it, says the Taoist, how can one claim to offer rules for good living? How can one ever feel confident enough in his own knowledge to do such a thing? The cocksure person who pretends to know so much is probably pretending just for the sake of his own ego. The person who is truly wise is the one who does not know that he is wise. Thinking that we know, when actually we do not, is a special sickness to which all men are prone. Only when we become sick of such conceit and fraud can we cure ourselves of the sickness.

In his desire to help people do this, Chuang-tse often used the light touch of humor. He tells the story of how he once dreamed that he was a butterfly, fluttering around gaily here and there. He was completely unaware of being a man any longer. Then suddenly, he awoke and found himself lying in bed, still a human being. However, Chuang-tse then had to ask himself: "Was I then a man dreaming I was a butterfly, or am I now a butterfly dreaming I am a man?"

What is truth? How do I know that I know? These are questions which cannot be answered definitely by the true wise man, though many self-styled sages offer answers. All answers depend upon a time and a place and a situation. The man of Tao forgets lists of answers; he ignores codes of behavior; he rises above morals and ethics. The man of Tao does not submit to external authorities of any sort. He merely listens keenly to his own deepest nature. In doing so, he not only finds truth but also lives truth. For in his deepest nature, there is the Tao, operating clearly and strongly. Without going out of his door, the man of Tao can know the whole world.

Such were the words of the pioneers of Taoism, who would have preferred not to talk at all. They knew that their impressions of life could not best be conveyed in words. Their impressions would be fully understood only by those who shared them as a result of their own experiences. Each of us has at some time failed in the attempt to put his deepest feelings or intuitions into words. In such moments, we may express ourselves in poetry, or music, or some other art form. It is just so with the Taoists. If we are to understand them, we must realize that we are dealing with the poetry of their impressions. Words are not meant to be taken literally, since words cannot convey impressions adequately. But the words of Taoism are meant to be taken seriously.

Taoism as a Religious Cult

The Taoists' reluctance to use words as a vehicle for their feelings was not misplaced. Hardly were the words uttered or the symbols drawn on the paper, when the weakness of words betrayed the speakers and the writers. People took the words literally, and they followed them to the letter, like the codes that the earlier Taoists so ridiculed. In clinging to the descriptions of the man of Tao, people forgot the inward harmony that had first been described. In memorizing the "three treasures," people neglected to find them buried within themselves. In trying to follow Lao-tse and Chuang-tse exactly, people lost their way to understanding the Tao.

This is not at all surprising. The people of Lao-tse's time were never really lifted from their superstitious ways by his utterances, or those of any other teacher. Their worlds were filled with daily concerns for work and friends and families. It was easy and reassuring to placate the ever-present "spirits" who were everywhere about them. These people did not have the time, the education, or the desire to think searchingly about their lives. Most people, everywhere, and in every age, live their lives without thinking deeply about them.

Even so, most people have a high respect for those who do think deeply, and especially for those few famous thinkers whose ideas appeal to them as being an important part of what is universally true. Often, out of their respect, they turn to veneration and then, almost imperceptibly, to worship. Thus it was with Lao-tse. Later generations regarded him as a god. They forgot that the happiness of which he spoke had to be reached by the process he had followed—

conforming to the way of all things—the Tao. They seemed to think that there were short cuts to the contentment that Lao-tse had experienced.

Gradually through the years, the self-knowledge and life-knowledge that had been the goals of Taoism got left behind. Newer Taoists sprang up, whose major concerns lay in the banishing of cares and sorrows. True, the earlier Taoists had wanted this, too, but as a by-product of harmony with the nature of things. Now the Taoists wished to make happiness an easier thing. And they began to offer pills and potions and magical rituals to help in achieving it.

Taoism became a search for the magical elixir, a cure for all ills, and a prolonger of carefree life. The early Taoists had at first retreated from the artificial and unnatural in order to know reality. They were followed, centuries later, by Taoists who retreated from reality in order to follow superstitious customs they hoped would bring escape from unhappiness. The earlier Taoists had prized the knowledge and understanding of the Tao, seeking to fit in with the nature of things. The later Taoists tried to interfere with natural processes, in order to gain immortality and freedom from care.

Other Taoists, despairing of this life, have become hermits and live merely for death, following what they believe to be the correct interpretation of Lao-tse's teaching to "do nothing." They are few in number, for the masses of the people cling to the more popular expression of Taoism— the superstitious and magical. The Taoists accept their religion for the comfort they receive now and for the hope it gives them for their future after death.

Lao-tse taught that men should neither worry about nor serve the spirits which many thought to be all about them. Instead, they should study to learn the ways of the world. Nothing could come from their ignorant and fearful worship of such spirits. The man of Tao was not troubled by spirits, either good or bad. Those who worked magic tried to force nature to do their wills. And force was never successful. Nature could teach them this.

Lao-tse, looking on the present scene, would doubtless be distressed that this had come to pass from what he had taught. He would be filled with the sense of futility that would come to any prophet who could look upon what had developed out of his labors. The religion which looks to Lao-tse as founder is full of all the things he considered least worth-while.

This new Taoism could not survive as an effective religion, even as the old Taoism had not lasted. Gradually, the people who had been attracted to the thoughtfulness of Taoism became discouraged. The people who had sought the betterment of human society turned to Confucianism, which offered more direct and practical help in that problem. Those who had liked the meditative aspects of Taoism began to investigate Buddhism. And classical Taoism, as Lao-tse taught it, practically ceased to exist.

The religion of the average Chinese person today is a blend of different religious traditions. Taoism's role in that blend has been a light-hearted and playful facet in the national life. Most of the religious holidays, with their gay ceremonies, had their origin in the past of Taoism. These include ceremonies for certain significant birthdays—especially those of boys—ceremonies for marriage, for the birth of children, and for some seasons of the year. There is now a group of trained priests who minister to those who call themselves Taoists.

Lao-tse's and Chuang-tse's Taoism lives on mostly in the things it offered to other stronger and longer-lived religions. Confucianism added the Taoist belief in the basic goodness of people. Buddhism in China, with its already strong emphasis on the importance of knowing the inner self, was strengthened and changed somewhat by this native religion. As a religious philosophy, Taoism faded, but it did send many away with the understanding that the inner life of the self was the life that was important.

11. Confucianism: The Way of Harmony and Propriety

LEGENDS say that when Lao-tse was very old he was visited by a scholarly young man from a nearby province. The young man, who spent most of his days in study, had come to ask some questions. Like Lao-tse, he was concerned with the quality of life in China. He, too, believed that back in the "good old days" of the Golden Age people had lived better lives and the country as a whole was more prosperous.

This young man was Confucius, and he had arrived at those beliefs via the route of much study and research into the ancient literature of China. As he collected and translated the literary Classics, he found what he considered to be clues to the happier life of the earlier days. For a real understanding of Confucian philosophy, we still turn to his comments upon those Classics. The Analects, stories about Confucius and his comments upon life situations, also tell of his proposals for the good of his countrymen.

Both Lao-tse and Confucius were concerned with the social and moral weaknesses of their generation. Lao-tse met the challenge of life with the radical view that the institutions and customs of his day were unnatural and thus to be avoided. Confucius, a true conservative, taught that the best from the past should be kept and properly improved. In the past lay the key to the present and the future. He did not seek to start either a new religion or a new system of ethics.

Confucius was facing the same basic questions that concerned Lao-tse. "What is life all about? How can I get along best in the world? How can I live a happy life? What am I?" For part of the answer, Confucius turned to nature and the Tao, as Lao-tse had done. All parts of nature, he observed, operate in harmony with one another. He decided that men might learn from nature. By following the way of nature and harmony, men would do the best thing they could in the world.

Harmony, then, was Confucius' ideal, just as it was Lao-tse's. Wherein lay the difference between the two men?

For one thing, their personalities were very different. In all the problems they faced, the dissimilarity of their outlooks determined the differences in the solutions they gave. While Lao-tse tended to be an "individualist," Confucius believed that man's entire responsibility was social. Man was not man apart from his fellows. Harmony for man, therefore, meant harmony with other men. Lao-tse believed that man's responsibility was to understand himself and to get himself directly in harmony with the Tao. But Confucius believed that man's responsibility was to co-operate with others and to perform the duties society expected of him. Such co-operation was rooted, of course, in the Tao, but the human level of experience was the medium through which human beings expressed their belonging to the universe. When a person developed his capacity for harmony with his fellow human beings, then he could understand universal harmony.

The Need for Rules for Living

Confucius saw that not all men were conducting themselves in such co-operative, mutually helpful ways. This, to Confucius' practical mind, meant simply that they needed some definite standards. In his writings, Confucius emphasized such standards, repeating and interpreting the ancient, traditional rules of Chinese society. He saw no need to add new rules. His duty as he saw it was to compile and transmit to posterity the literature describing the old customs and manners of Chinese society. He wrote no new things, for he believed and loved the ancients.

Why was it that rules were needed? All the rules arose originally out of human needs. This is the way all good laws come about. There are problems in living together, and rules are designed to solve the problems. Wherever there are many people living together, there are more problems than where there are few. The government of a large city is much more complex than the government of a tiny village. China already had many people. And thanks mainly to Confucius, she has accumulated many rules. All these rules are attempts to make life go more smoothly. They are not to be enforced like traffic regulations. They are more like rules of etiquette.

Rules have more meaning when they are specific. People who like to live in an ordered society feel more comfortable when the rules for society are available in definite order and when they designate times and places. So it was that, through the years, Confucianists placed great value on numerous lists of specific rules covering everything from passing the time of day with a friend to worshiping the ancestors. Dress and conversation were prescribed. Even posture and steps were listed, so that no one who was sincere in his efforts could fail to do the right thing. Following the rules showed a person's real desire to co-operate with his fellow men.

How to Get Along with Other People: The Superior Man

In order that people might know how they ought to live, Confucius described a "Superior Man," or a noble or princely man. Confucius called him a "princely" or superior man because of his belief that the rulers were teachers. However, anyone at any time can live as a Superior Man.

The Superior Man has developed within his personality Five Constant Virtues, which he has practiced until they are as natural as breathing. Doing the right thing is an inseparable part of him. When Confucius said of himself that not until he was seventy years of age could he follow the promptings of his heart without overstepping the boundaries of right, perhaps he was being overly modest or very humble. Nevertheless, a good Confucianist spends as long as it takes to make the right way of living so habitual that he will not have to stop to think about doing the right thing.

(1) Right Attitude. The first of the Five Constant Virtues concerns attitude. The Superior Man desires to be in harmony with other men. He knows that he cannot fulfill his role in life unless he is co-operative and accommodating. The right attitude is revealed through conduct. People have the seed of such an attitude within them, but it must be helped to develop. This virtuous attitude is sometimes thought of as an inner law of self-control.

(2) Right Procedure. The second Constant Virtue is proper procedure. The man of noble mind has made a study of the rules of conduct. He has learned how to apply them to every incident he faces. He knows all the rules for etiquette, which set forth what each social situation requires of the completely humanized person. He knows all the ceremonies and rituals centering around an-

cestor reverence. He knows how to sit, how to stand, how to converse, how to walk, and how to control his facial expressions on all occasions. Yet all these rituals and procedures are without value if a man does not have the proper attitude. "A man without charity in his heart, what has he to do with ceremonies?"

(3) *Right Knowledge.* The third Constant Virtue is knowledge. The Superior Man is a knowing man, for a person must be educated in order to respond in the exact way. The Confucianists' goal is to grow gradually from memorized rules to habits. The subjects that teach a person correct moral habits are the history, literature, and civics that make up the Chinese *Classics.* The Superior Man plans his education to include all such essentials. For centuries, the *Classics* were the bases of education in China. Modern times have substituted other subjects, but the Confucianist still holds the *Classics* in respect.

When Confucius stressed the importance of education, he was not suggesting a new idea. He was repeating and emphasizing what the ancients had said. The social order depends upon fundamental morality—the morality of proper words and actions. Also like the ancients, Confucius believed that morality was to be applied in all levels of life, but in a very significant way to the ruling level. For the rulers were the teachers of all. They taught the needed morality most effectively when they set a good moral example and when they governed kindly. Only through such a process would the new Golden Age finally arrive, when all men would deal with each other in kindness and consideration.

(4) *Right Moral Courage.* According to the fourth Constant Virtue, the Superior Man should develop the moral courage necessary to remain loyal to himself and charitable toward his neighbors. His character is such that everything he does makes a worth-while contribution to society. Through his every deed, human relationships are improved.

(5) *Right Persistence.* The last of the Five Constant Virtues was an emphasis of their title—constancy. The Superior Man has achieved the other four virtues, and he persists in his achievement. He is unfailingly kind and helpful. He knows what his duty is on each occasion, and he always knows how to do that duty. Because he has developed the seeds of virtue within his nature, he is in

harmony with everything in the universe. Because he has harmony within himself, he is part of cosmic harmony. That is why he is able to do the right thing at the right time always.

Perfect Humanity

Confucianists often speak of "perfect humanity." It can be achieved by a person because of something the Confucianists believe to be present within each person, even at birth. This is a native goodness or kindly love that can be developed through feelings of helpfulness toward others. It was Mencius, the best-known Confucianist of a later period, who emphasized the native goodness of men. When he and Confucius spoke of man's goodness, they meant that he was fit to live with other people—in the long run. There was quite a course of preparation first, as we have seen. Behavior, habits, thought patterns, and judgments had to be improved.

When a man has educated himself to be a Superior Man, he can be kind, helpful, and good. The "seed" of goodness within him makes these qualities possible. So many good acts are possible that the Chinese despaired of ever listing them all one by one. Their "Golden Rule" is stated in negative terms. Nevertheless, it is full of concern for others. "Do not unto others what you would not they should do unto you."

Right Relationships

As part of their effort to make right living easy for everyone, Confucianists have stressed five important personal relationships that require kindness and tact. These were once taught to every schoolboy, but that system of education was discontinued early in this century. Still, many Confucianists think that if everyone used the Five Constant Virtues in these five relationships, a true golden age would begin. If happiness or harmony is to exist, the ten people involved in these contacts must use virtuous attitudes and conduct toward each other:

(a) Husband and wife
(b) Father and son
(c) Elder brother and younger brother
(d) Ruler and subject
(e) Friend and friend

Notice that something is expected of both parties to the relationship. Each is responsible for acting and speaking and thinking in kind and helpful ways.

Some may say that this does not go far enough. What about other people of their own and other lands? Confucianists do hold to the ideal of charity and kindness to all one's neighbors and to all other persons on earth. But one individual does not come in contact with *all* other persons. His circle of acquaintances is limited. It is for this reason that the five personal relationships are listed. It is much better for a person to act with kindness and regard for the few persons he contacts frequently than to mouth words about "loving" all men. He will never know all men. A good life consists of acting properly toward the persons one meets daily in everyday experiences.

Family Love and Devotion

Long before the point where history books begin, the Chinese believed that one of the first duties a person has is to his parents. In the large families of the Chinese custom, parents, grandparents, and great-grandparents are looked upon as very wise, much beloved, and greatly revered. Their deaths do not lessen the respect that is paid to them. Reverence for ancestors is a way of extending the "family feeling" beyond death. Confucius and Confucianists have played a major part in keeping loyal devotion to parents uppermost in the ideals of China.

Children in China have never been allowed the freedom of choice and behavior that we know in the West. They are disciplined kindly but firmly from the start, in order that their attitudes and behavior may be proper. Disobedience has been very rare, and disrespect even rarer. Children carry their devotion to parents to the point of accepting parents' decisions for them, including the choice of a husband or a wife. The Chinese believe that in such matters the parents are far wiser than their children.

Naturally, family loyalty has changed rapidly with the other changes of the twentieth century. New political developments have already caused some breakdowns of the old family traditions and may cause greater changes yet. However, filial piety has been a part of Chinese life for so long a time that it is still an influence in China.

Ancestor Reverence

Confucius encouraged ancestor reverence or worship because he believed that it helped a person to develop proper attitudes and conduct. When a person offers gifts before a plaque in memory of a departed ancestor, he remembers his origin and his love. This experience draws from him feelings of respect and loyalty. For a person to carry filial piety beyond death shows an even greater degree of devotion than simply to honor living parents.

Many Confucianists offered gifts and sacrifices in honor of the dead without ever believing that the spirits of the dead were present. Confucianists found it worth-while because it helped them to build good habits of respect for others. At the same time, this adds strength to society. For these two reasons, Confucianism includes ancestor reverence among the important aspects of human behavior.

Ways of Worship

Confucius did not seek to change or even to say much about the religious beliefs and practices of his day. He simply accepted them as they were—*in so far as they served society*. He was not in the least interested in popular religious ideas or customs that ignored common experiences and knowledge. He did not like to speak of the spirits that so many people worshiped out of superstition and fear. Once Confucius said to a student who asked about spirits, "While you are not able to serve men, how can you serve their spirits?" To him, it was a waste of time to concern yourself with anything you could not definitely know. Life after death was another example. "While you do not know life, how can you know about death?" One had no time for things he could not know, since knowing even his neighbors required a lifetime.

Confucius was not concerned with ideas about God and other problems in theology. But he had a real devotion to the ancient religious ceremonies, because be believed that they helped to build the habits and attitudes necessary to proper conduct. His personal religion was limited to reverence of ancestors, the moral life of the Five Constant Virtues, and recognition and reverence of a just Heaven above. For the most part, Confucius passed on the ancient

Chinese religion, which was a blend of reverence for nature gods and ancestors.

Large numbers of the Chinese people worship Heaven as a supreme god or as one of many gods, with interpretations as varied as those given to any other god. The worship of the Heaven-god has been an imperial worship, administered throughout Chinese history by the Emperor with seasonal ceremonies. Very few Confucianists, along with other educated Chinese, actively joined in worshiping Heaven. However, they tended to support the imperial ceremonies as being worth-while because they might help people to remember their origin.

Many people have asked: Is Confucianism a religion? Confucius himself did not claim that what he was teaching was religion. He did not expect a revelation from Heaven as authority for what he taught. He told his followers that it was good to be in awe of Heaven because it was an intelligent, creating force that moved in a perfectly natural way, through the Tao. Heaven was impartial and just. Later Confucianists added the belief that Heaven was a personal god, but one who exerted no influence on men or on the world he created. Still the major focus of Confucianism has always been on humanity. Mencius described the will of Heaven in terms of what it means to men by saying that being true to its nature is Heaven's way. Trying to be true to his nature should also be the way of men.

Confucius considered himself to be a social reformer, rather than a religious leader. He dreamed of and worked for a society in which men would live in perfect harmony. If what he taught was not religion, it was at least religious. Confucius taught his beliefs because he believed they were backed by the nature of things. His teaching was an attempt to get man in line with reality.

The Place of Confucius in Chinese History

In his lifetime, Confucius was a respected teacher, but he was one teacher among many. While he lived, his fame and popularity were never sufficient to result in the adoption of his teachings in government. On the contrary, he spent long years in trying to persuade one ruler after another to adopt his ideas, all in vain. He had some loyal students who were convinced of the superiority of his ideas, but other people did not wholly agree in this opinion. It was not until several hundred years after his death that Confucius' teachings on morality began to gain an important place in the life of the Chinese.

The Chinese *Classics*, in which he had invested so much time and thought, were made the basis of civil-service examinations for governmental positions. This marked the time when the whole pattern of Chinese life began to be Confucian. For over two thousand years, Confucian thought dominated education, government, and culture. This officially was brought to an end shortly after the beginning of this century, but people move more slowly than institutions. All the people have not abruptly forgotten the old traditions.

Confucius' personal ideals never reached fullest flowering, even though they helped to shape the course of Chinese civilization. Sometimes rulers and politicians seemed to be more sincere than they actually were in following his teachings of morality, hoping that their apparent loyalty to Confucius would gain favor from the people. Sometimes they heaped titles and honors upon him posthumously or upon his descendants.

Immediately following his death, Confucius was worshiped as an ancestor by members of his family. Others joined in the reverence, because in China a great teacher is given the same respect as a parent. It was always his teachings that interested his admirers, never any magical deeds or superhuman qualities. Confucius has been worshiped as a god, but this was the worship of the unschooled people, who believe that the important thing is to worship plentifully, not thoughtfully. Perhaps this kind of worship could be described as a special hero worship. In general, Confucius has been to China—and to a lesser extent to Japan—the great teacher. He has been honored far above any other man in the whole of his country's history.

Confucianism as a Religious Cult

At times strong attempts have been made to establish Confucianism as a state religion, with Confucius as a sort of savior. These efforts have failed for several reasons. First of all, the Chinese have always been accustomed to religious freedom, and the idea of a single state religion offended them. Secondly, they seemed unwilling to turn Confucianism into a religion like Taoism and Buddhism.

Perhaps it had been with them too long as the broad base of their lives for them to limit it to an organized religion.

New political movements in China have sometimes blamed Confucianism and Confucius for many of the ills of Chinese society. This is partly due to their attempt to discredit old traditions and beliefs, in order to bring in new ideas of government and education. Today, Confucius does not hold the same respected place in the memories and the history of his people.

What Does Life Require of Men?

Though his teachings were never to achieve the success Confucius wished for them, some of his important ideas survived his death and the intervening centuries. These ideas have made a distinctive contribution to China and to its neighbor nation, Japan, which has so often found China's thoughts and art worth borrowing. In fact, the life and thought of the kindly philosopher have contributed to the knowledge of the whole world.

Above all, Confucianism calls for an intense concern for humanity. Confucianists' main argument with both Buddhists and Taoists has been that they turned their backs on their fellow men to go seeking after what was best for them personally. Never, never, should self come before society. A person finds his fulfillment in the very act of helping and knowing others.

Confucianism demands of rulers and leaders a special accounting to the people they rule. The only reason rulers exist is to help people to be better. If this idea could ever be accepted seriously by the leaders of nations, statesmanship would attain new heights, and life for all would be improved. Finally, say Confucianists, even world peace would be achieved.

Who can say all the good that might result if families would accept the charge Confucius gave them? Confucianism places before the family the importance of the family's job in moral education. It points out how natural and cheerful the moral approach to life is.

"What does life ask of me?" China has traditionally said: "It asks kind attitudes and conduct. It asks that you live with the interests of your fellow men uppermost in your concerns. In so living with others, you will gain the greatest good—you will find your place in the world. You will find yourself."

Section Four

THE RELIGION OF JAPAN

12. Shinto: The Way of the Gods

THERE are many people who think that Shinto, the native religion of the Japanese, no longer exists, or that it is rapidly dying. They think it began to decline with Japan's surrender at the end of the Second World War. But traditional beliefs and customs have a way of living on. It is never possible to decree or legislate faith out of existence. Japan's defeat in World War II and the American occupation for some years following have undoubtedly changed some religious ceremonies and practices. Still there is something that cannot be changed. It is the underlying religious spirit of the Japanese. They call it Shinto, the "way of the gods."

The Japanese share the Oriental respect for their cultural inheritance. In the last hundred years, this reverence for the past has been put to the strongest test one could imagine. Japan has survived what amounted to a revolution—the onslaught of Western industrialization and ideas, and two world wars, one of which led to crushing defeat. No other country has had to move so rapidly from feudalism into industrialism. Yet her people still meet each day with an appreciation of its beauty, a strong respect for each other, and a deep devotion to their country.

It is true that Japanese ideas are changing. But since Japan's history has shown more flux during the past eighty years than in the previous thousand, it is difficult to chart the changes. We must remember that the future comes from the present, as the present was derived from the past. Therefore, it is safe to assume that the values dearest to the Japanese will go with them into the future.

Kinship with Nature

A Japanese would probably ask, "What is life?" The question "What is my life?" would not occur to him. He sees himself as only part of the living, inspiring wonder of everything that exists. He has a feeling of nearness to na-

ture that the average European or American does not have.
The Japanese have always felt the lure of the outdoor
spaces—the sand, the wind, the stars, the waves, the hum
of the insects, the music of a waterfall.

The Japanese believe that the same wonderful forces
that move in nature move in themselves. There is no difference. There is no dividing line between divine and human. For this reason, a person's religion and his life have
entered into each other so that it is almost impossible to
tell where one begins and the other ends. Those who claim
that Shinto is not a religion are probably confused by this
tendency. To the thoughtful Japanese, this is as it should
be. Why should religion be something "added onto" a
person's life?

The Japanese find comfort and inspiration in the beauties of their surroundings. They have built their shrines in
spots of breath-taking beauty. They try to keep themselves constantly attuned to the loveliness all about them:

> E'en in a single leaf of a tree
> Or a tender blade of grass,
> The awe-inspiring Deity
> Manifests Itself.

The practice of beauty leads the Japanese to participate
in ceremonies and festivals that may seem strange to us.
The Insect-Hearing Festival is an example of this. On a
quiet evening in the early weeks of autumn, the emperor
and thousands of his subjects sit quietly and listen to the
noises of various insects. Just as typical is the story of the
Zen Buddhist teacher who stepped before his class one day
to give a lecture. He paused to listen to the song of a bird
outside the window, and then he dismissed the class.
There are sermons in nature—and the Japanese hear them
freely.

At the time of the blossoming of the cherry trees, the
Japanese often close their shops and go to the parks and
to the country, to enjoy the beauty of the blossoms before
they fall. Sometimes they spend evenings gazing at the
moon. Or they will sit for hours contemplating the beauty
of a garden, or a flower arrangement, or even a single twig
or leaf.

Admiring the beauty about them has led them to cultivate beauty in their own homes and yards and in all their

arts and crafts. Painstakingly they have sought to capture the inspiration that life and nature offer them. Sometimes they use poems to express their feeling of kinship with nature.

Usually, the Japanese write poetry that is quite short, with just enough description to convey their feelings. Often, of course, their poetry does not impart the same feelings to someone else, particularly a reader from another country. But one interprets for himself. Who is to say what a poem ought to mean?

Here are several examples of Japanese nature poetry, which may mean as much or as little as the reader can find in them:

> On the plum blossoms
> Thick fell the snow;
> I wished to gather some
> To show to thee,
> But it melted in my hands.

> Among the hills
> The snow still lies —
> But the willows
> Where the torrents rush together
> Are in full bud.

> To what shall I compare
> This life of ours?
> It is like a boat
> Which at daybreak rows away
> And leaves no trace behind it.

> The sky is a sea
> Where the cloud-billows rise;
> And the moon is a bark;
> To the groves of the stars
> It is oaring its way.[1]

The Importance of Purity

The sky, the flowers, the trees, and the beautiful land speak to the Japanese of beauty and purity. For centuries, the Japanese have looked upon such sights with reverence.

[1] From *A History of Japanese Literature* by W. G. Aston. Reprinted by permission of the publishers, Appleton-Century-Crofts, Inc.

They have felt awe in the presence of the pure loveliness
of which they are so deeply aware. They have wished to
be worthy of it. This has prompted them to strive for
inner and outer purity.

A Japanese does not approach a shrine, whether in his
own home or in a public place, without first going through
a ceremony of cleansing. There are special water troughs
near the public shrines, from which a worshiper may dip
the water for washing his hands and rinsing his mouth.
Only after he has purified himself in this way does he think
himself worthy to worship at the shrine. Thoughtful Japanese realize that this is a symbol of inner purity, which
does not really depend on outward cleansing.

Japanese homes are models of cleanliness and order. The
god shelf—center of Shinto worship in the home—is kept
spotless. The shelters of the shrines are rebuilt frequently
so that no decay will mar the place of beauty.

In old Japan, there was a semi-annual observance called
the Great Purification. All the people took part in the
ceremony by rubbing slips of paper over their bodies and
then burning them or throwing them into a river, lake, or
ocean. Then the emperor, speaking for the Sun Goddess,
would pronounce all the people to be pure again. Long,
long ago, the ancient Japanese had probably believed that
cleanliness of body was important to the gods. Later Japanese came to think that the gods desired moral purity as
well. The Great Purification ceremonies are a symbol of
both.

Such ceremonies serve to make people feel right again
with themselves and with the world. Shintoists have considered it to be very important to hold the ceremonies
regularly, so that all may feel free of impurity. They do not
worry about personal sins or errors. They are so interested in all their people that they feel a shared guilt for
everyone's accumulated shortcomings and impurities. This
group guilt makes them seek purification for the whole
society of Japanese.

Devotion to Japan

The Japanese read the classical myths of the beginnings
of their land in the old "Chronicles of Japan," the *Nihongi*,
and "The Records of Ancient Matters," the *Kojiki*. They
read of how the Sun Goddess, Amaterasu, sent her grand-

son to be the first ruler of the islands. This is what she told him: "I think that this land will undoubtedly be suitable for the extension of the heavenly task, so that its glory should fill the universe. It is, doubtless, the center of the world."

This same high estimate of their country has been a first consideration of the Japanese people. They are passionately devoted to their beautiful islands. They work the soil with unlimited patience. They tend their gardens and parks and farms with loving skill.

Other peoples have long since become acquainted with the intense loyalty the Japanese have for their country, their countrymen, and their emperor. It stems from their feeling that they are the descendants of the gods, that their country is the land chosen by the gods, and that their emperor is the direct descendant of Amaterasu. This tradition, in addition to the fact that for centuries the Japanese lived almost isolated on their islands, has been largely responsible for the "spirit of Japan."

Each Japanese is interested in all Japanese. What is good for the whole of Japan is what each Japanese wishes for himself. The total welfare of the nation is involved. Their emperor reminds them of their divine descent and their responsibility to their nation. It is because of this that the Japanese were so devoted to the royal household, prior to the end of World War II.

To the Japanese loyalty is such a virtue that their soldiers have often sacrificed their lives without the slightest hesitation. In fact, they have sometimes been eager to do so, believing that their spirits would then help to protect their country. Partly, the emphasis upon courage and loyalty stems from the very recent feudal past of Japan, when knights were taught to be steadfast soldiers. Although feudalism has been replaced, this much has carried over into the present. Loyalty and honor still suggest divine attitudes to the Japanese.

Willingness to Learn

Their fervent interest in their own culture has not kept the Japanese from learning from other people. They have borrowed philosophy and ethics from Confucianists, religion and art from Buddhists, and industrial techniques from Westerners. But when trade in goods and ideas did come, Japan received them in her own way. On Japanese soil, these became Japanese.

In religion, the Japanese have learned much from what the Chinese Confucianists and Buddhists could teach them. But Shinto remains the religious-patriotic personality of the Japanese people. For a time, State Shinto—or Shrine Shinto—was taught in the schools in the form of certain ceremonials, and was administered by a special branch of the government. Recently this has been changed, and some of the seasonal festivals are no longer widely observed. Today, when a Japanese calls himself Shintoist, he may mean that he is a member of one of a number of Shinto sects. Or he may mean that he respects and reveres the traditions of the past as the "way of the gods" underlying even Buddhism or other religions.

The Goodness of Men

The Japanese find life very good, and they are glad to accept it as it is. They are not inclined to question it. They take life in a more joyous way than the followers of some religions. Even Buddhists in Japan do not dwell at much length on life's sorrow. Shintoists feel "at home" in the world. They believe that the gods desire their happiness and well-being. Life is good, and men are good. How could it be otherwise, when the gods have created them?

The Shinto religion has no list of commandments, no set of moral rules to be followed. More than 150 years ago, one Japanese scholar wrote: "It is because the Japanese were truly moral in their practice that they required no theory of morals, and the fuss made by the Chinese about theoretical morals is owing to their laxity in practice."

Another Japanese of the same period pointed out that human beings have been produced "by the spirit of the two Creative Deities" (Izanagi and Izanami). Therefore, they are naturally endowed with the knowledge of what they ought to do and what they ought to refrain from. "It is unnecessary for them to trouble their heads with systems of morality," he added.

Since the Japanese feel that human beings are really good, they have never worried about being sinful. Men may make mistakes, which might be called "sins," but they are not full of sin. A Japanese worships more through giving thanks than through reciting his shortcomings and seeking forgiveness for them. No Shintoist is taught to think of himself as "a worm in the dust."

Shintoists have never been concerned with an idea of an afterlife. There are no teachings about a life beyond the grave, and Shintoists do not pray for a future bliss. They pray for much more specific things such as food, happiness, the welfare of the nation, and to express thanks. Whatever Shinto lacks in not emphasizing a life beyond death, Buddhism has supplied to the Japanese people. The people in Japan, like the people in China, are inclined to combine teachings from various religions.

The Gods

Most Shintoists speak of "the gods." For the majority of Shintoists, there are many gods and goddesses, who represent all human interests and all phases of nature. Thoughtful Shintoists may speak of "the divine." To them, there is a divinity in all natural things—for there is nothing supernatural. This quality of the divine is in man as well, although he does not understand how it can be so. The reverence paid to many gods and to the spirits of heroes and famous men is simply a recognition of the divinity that is present in all life.

The more thoughtful persons in modern Japan have come to believe in one God. Or, they might explain it as a belief in one source for the divine quality of all life. But Shinto has largely thrived on the belief in many gods. Records from 901 A.D. tell of three thousand shrines in Japan, where over three thousand deities were worshiped. By 1914, there were over 190,000 shrines in Japan. Some of these were major shrines, visited by hundreds of thousands of people during a year. Others were simple wayside shrines in the outlying districts.

The Sun Goddess, Amaterasu, is the center of Shinto worship. Her brother, the Storm God, is widely honored, and so is the Food Goddess. All the gods are descendants of the original divine pair, who gave birth to the islands of Japan, as well as to the hosts of other deities. They are called Izanagi, the Sky Father, and Izanami, the Earth Mother. Japanese mythology fills in the details of the story of creation, including the account of how Izanagi ordered Amaterasu to rule over the Plain of High Heaven. For many years, Amaterasu has been the symbol of everything most precious in the development of the Japanese people.

At the time when Amaterasu dispatched her grandson to rule over Japan, she gave him the three most sacred objects in the Shinto religion. The imperial jewels, which are kept in the Tokyo palace, are symbols of obedience and gentleness. The sword, kept in the shrine at Owari, represents wisdom and justice. And the mirror, housed in the Ise shrine, symbolizes righteousness and purity. Shintoists have believed that the myths and objects serve to remind them of the divine mandate by which their emperors rule.

Shinto Worship

Since the recent war there have been dramatic changes in Japanese life and manners. It is impossible to predict how the ancient ceremonies of Shinto will be continued in the years ahead. The peace treaty signed between Japan and the United States and the withdrawal of occupation forces may lead to a re-emphasis on native Japanese culture. Or it may not. The emperor, by his own decree, has stated that he is no longer to be regarded as divinely descended from the Sun Goddess. Yet the habits and feelings of loyal Japanese subjects may have been barely affected by his statement.

The Japanese continue to go to the shrines of their different gods and goddesses, to pray for good crops or food or national prosperity. They cleanse themselves in the customary way and clap their hands to show respect, as Oriental people often do. Then they give an offering of money or rice, take off their shoes, and enter the prayer hall.

Shintoists use, not images of their gods, but symbols of them. On their god shelves are tablets or slips of paper on which are written the names of the gods they wish to honor. A light burns there, and the family places flowers and a bit of wine or rice cake there daily, if possible. Loyal Shintoists try to hold brief prayer ceremonies before the god shelf each day.

Shinto priests, who may live just as other men do, lead official services on important religious days. They do not preach at regular services each week. They are responsible for protecting the sacred objects in the shrines. Frequently they have another occupation besides the priesthood.

Shinto shrines have a special gateway, called a *torii*. No one knows exactly how this attractive structure came to be a part of the shrines; its real origin is lost in antiquity. Probably it was used years ago for hanging the birds that were offered as a sacrifice to the Sun Goddess. Although it no longer serves that purpose, yet a *torii* stands at the entrance to every Shinto shrine. Sometimes there is a row of them. The *torii* is a distinctive symbol of the Shinto religion.

Shinto Sects

The Shinto shrines or "churches" found in other countries are not part of State Shinto but sectarian forms of Shinto. We might call them denominations. They are not state-supported and do not depend upon the favor of the Japanese emperor. American-Japanese followers usually prefer not to refer to these movements by the name Shinto.

Most of the sects, however, incorporate into their teachings and rites many elements of State Shinto and of Buddhism as well. In Japan, thirteen such sects are officially recognized; but there are many others not officially listed. Many of them have adopted the educational and missionary methods of Christian denominations. Some of them center about the worship of an all-powerful, universal God. Some stress faith-healing.

The religious answers of the old "spirit of Japan" remain a force to consider in the religious life of the world today. The Japanese have found deep satisfaction for themselves. They have suggested that others might find similar satisfaction through simply accepting life as it is and appreciating it for the beauties and wonders it offers the person who takes time to see and hear.

Section Five

THE SEMITIC RELIGIONS

JUDAISM

13. The Lord Is One

THE WHOLE WORLD knows the Jews. Their wanderings have carried them over the earth. With them they have taken their religion, to which most of them have remained intensely loyal. When the sun sets at the beginning of the Sabbath, many millions of Jews start their day of rest and worship. Their numbers are not large in comparison with the world's total population. But the mark that the Jews have made in the world is large and significant indeed.

Judaism is the "mother religion" of both Christianity and Islam. These three have been the major religions of the Western parts of the world. From Judaism, Christianity and Islam "inherited" many religious ideas, morals, and practices. If a historian ignored the contribution of the Jews to the development of Western civilization, he could not write its past or understand its present.

Jews do not belong to one race of people. Their wanderings over the earth have made this impossible. Thousands of years ago, they were a group of tribes, then called the Hebrews. Now the term "Jew" applies correctly to anyone who is a member of the Jewish faith. Nationally speaking, Jews are Germans, Arabian, American, and almost everything else.

Despite their widespread national homes, the Jews have retained throughout the ages a sense of closeness to one another. They have done this by following carefully their religious practices and laws. They have done it through a single-minded insistence on the truth of what they call the Shema: "Hear, O Israel, the Lord our God, the Lord is One." This is the heart of every Jewish religious service. More than this, it is the heart of Judaism.

The One God

The Hebrews of ancient times sought to understand the meaning and purpose of life, just as did the ancient wise men of India and China. Out of that wondering, some

Hebrew of long ago came to feel a special relationship to the heart of the universe. Jewish traditions say that this man was Abraham. Abraham believed in a personal god who took a special interest in his destiny and dreams. Jews still honor this legendary man as the father of their people. Others took up his beliefs and found in them answers to their own questions about the world.

Eventually there appeared another great personality, Moses. He sharpened and clarified the idea of a personal god. He believed that the god had made a special agreement with Abraham and with all his descendants. They had promised their loyalty and devotion. In turn, the god would make them a mighty nation.

Traditional Jews still believe that God revealed the laws of life to Moses on Mount Sinai. They call Moses the founder of their religion. To him they give the credit for their important collection of laws on religious practice, behavior, and diet. He was the leader chosen by God to deliver the Hebrews from slavery in a strange country into a land of their own.

Such beliefs are based on the old, old tales found in the books of *Genesis* and *Exodus*. As many Jewish scholars have always been ready to point out, they cannot be taken as literal history. They are legends that were finally put into writing after centuries of existence in the memories of the Hebrew people, who had told them aloud generation after generation. The legends show that the god was at first a tribal god, a protector and benefactor of the Hebrews, the descendants of Abraham. He was known and worshiped by Abraham, his son Isaac, and his grandson Jacob, who was later called Israel.

Gradually, the Hebrew-Jewish people became convinced that this tribal god was actually the one and only God of all creation. Of course, this process took time. It took century after century, through the periods of the great Hebrew leaders—the tribal fathers, Moses, David and the other kings, Isaiah and the rest of the prophets. Slowly the people were gaining a world view that could not have been theirs at their beginning as wandering nomad tribes.

But now, for 2500 years, the great affirmation of Judaism has been: ". . . the Lord our God, the Lord is One." The development of the Jewish worship of one God reflects the experiences and temperament unique to the Jews. In their own way, they early arrived at a conclusion shared by all

major living religions today: underlying the endless variety
we see in life is a single purpose, a single reality.

For a long time, Jews did not find it important to dis-
cuss the nature of God. God exists, he is One, he is reality.
Even today, there is not a creed describing the characteristics of God. The *Shema* is sufficient.

However, some rabbis and philosophers did become interested in describing God's qualities, though no Jew is
ever required to affirm the ideas. God is righteous. He is
the Creator. He is Spirit. God is a sympathetic helper to
man, providing the means whereby man may save himself
from the limitations of ignorance and sinfulness. God has
made men as his children; thus, they reflect his nature.

Righteousness

No Jew can be said to love God, unless he is also in loving relationship with his neighbor. His neighbor includes
the alien and stranger in his land, whom he is asked to
treat as he treats his own people. Even more than this is a
Jew asked to do: ". . . thou shalt love they neighbor as
thyself."

Long after this was written, someone offered a challenge
to the famous Rabbi Hillel, who lived and taught at about
the same time as Jesus. The challenger asked the rabbi to
tell everything important about Judaism in the space of
time in which a man could stand on one foot. Rabbi Hillel
declared: "That which is hurtful to thee do not to thy
neighbor. This is the whole doctrine. The rest is commentary. Now go forth and learn."

Righteousness is so important to Jews that one might
say there are twin Jewish concerns—the oneness of God
and the righteousness of man. It is not hard for men to
follow the laws and will of God. Being made in God's
image, we have a natural capacity for goodness. Failure to
do the right, say Jews, is a denial of our own nature.

The Law

Often Jews have known God as the Lawgiver for their
people. The Law he gave is called the *Torah*, which means
"Teaching." The *Torah* consists of five books, sometimes
called the *Pentateuch*. The books are *Genesis, Exodus,
Leviticus, Numbers,* and *Deuteronomy*. All Jews are en-

couraged to study them. The complete *Torah* is regularly read each year in the synagogues, a portion on each Sabbath.

The *Torah* contains the legends of its own origin. According to these legends, God gave the Law to Moses on Mount Sinai, while the Hebrews were camping in the wilderness after escaping from Egypt. There the Hebrews renewed their agreement with God, promising to abide by his laws. Traditions further tell that there God spoke the Ten Commandments, which are found in the twentieth chapter of *Exodus*.

There were more commandments than these, to be sure —over six hundred in all. The commandments deal with a wealth of subjects: diet, crime and punishment, religious practices, holy days, and human relationships. Many Jews are among the first to insist that all these laws could not have been made in one time and one place. They are actually a collection of laws that the Hebrew-Jewish people formulated over a period of years of living together.

In the Jewish Bible, there is a second section known as "The Prophets." Many people believe that the height of Jewish thought and understanding was reached in the teachings of the prophets. The prophets did not foretell the future; they did "tell for" God. They were, first and foremost, spokesmen for God, who warned of dire consequences if God's will were not followed.

It was the prophets who tried to show the people that devotion to God did not lie solely in following each law in smallest detail. Why should a man concern himself with the detailed observance of over six hundred laws? Devotion lay in keeping the spirit of the Law.

According to Isaiah, these are attributes of the man who has pondered the spirit of the law:

> He who walks uprightly, and speaks sincerely,
> Who scorns the gain that is won by oppression,
> Who keeps his hand free from the touch of a bribe,
> Who stops his ears against hearing of bloodshed,
> And closes his eyes against looking on evil.

The prophet Micah reduced the important rules to only three, in his famous declaration of a man's spiritual duty:

You have been told, O man, what is good,
And what the Lord requires of you:
Only to do justice, and to love kindness,
And to walk humbly with your God.

For Amos, this was the spirit of the Law: "Seek the
Lord, that you may live."

Still a third section of the Jewish Bible is known as "The
Writings." It includes books of history recounting the ad-
ventures of the Hebrew-Jewish people and their growing
understanding of their world. It includes the Psalms and
the other books of poetry. While these are not considered
to be the basic Law, as the first five books are, they are
still in the spirit of the Law.

Modern Jews do not rely only on these three sections
of their sacred writing. There is another group of writings,
not a part of their Bible, but revered just second to it. This
is the Talmud. The Talmud is, in effect, an extension of
the Torah down into the centuries which followed the
completion of the other writings. The Talmud arose to
meet conditions that the Jews faced in later times. As their
homes and surroundings changed, their religious and cultural needs changed. Additional laws grew out of the
newer needs. These were passed from generation to generation by word of mouth. From time to time, learned
rabbis commented on these oral laws and on the earlier,
written ones, seeking to reinterpret them for the changing
times.
Through such continued commentary on past traditions
and laws in the light of newer situations, the Law of Judaism has remained alive. Modern Jews are able to adjust
themselves creatively to demands never dreamed of by
Moses or other great teachers of long ago.

The Jewish Task

The old tradition of the special agreement between God
and the Hebrews convinced many Jews that God had
chosen them as his favorites above all people on the earth.
They felt that they were privileged, and some of them
looked upon other peoples as inferior. However, later
teachers interpreted the idea of "chosenness" in a different

way. They said that the Jews had been chosen to serve the Lord, teaching others about the one God of all the world.

Still some Jews persisted in thinking in terms of exclusiveness. This caused the prophets much concern. Listen to an early prophet as he tries to correct their mistaken ideas:

> "Are you not like the Ethiopians in my sight,
>   O Israelites"; is an oracle of the Lord.
> "Did I not bring up Israel from the land of Egypt,
>   Also the Philistines from Caphtor, and the Syrians from Kir?"

An anonymous prophet shows that their God is the God of all people. He quotes God as saying: "Blessed be Egypt my people, and Assyria the work of my hands, and Israel my heritage." The whole book of Jonah is directed against narrow nationalism and the "chosen people" idea held by many Jews of that time.

There have always been many Jews who followed the emphasis of the prophets. These Jews have never believed themselves to be divinely chosen above all other peoples. Jews traditionally have been tolerant of believers in other faiths. Their patience and forbearance in matters of religion are close to the attitudes of sincere Hindus and Buddhists.

In their ideas of God and in their Law, the Jews find their dearest values. For these, they feel richly blessed. But most of them do not believe that the blessing is available only to them. Other people find values in their own ideas, too, and Jews accept such differences as enriching. For their part, Jews do not wish to persuade others to their religion. It is not a way of salvation. It is a way of life. And though there are numbers of converts to Judaism, Jews never work actively for the conversion of others.

The Kingdom of God

Jews are always concerned about righteousness. They have never felt that governments or societies, as people have known them, are as good as they could be. So the Jews look for a future time when all men will be righteous and when their families and societies will reflect that righteousness. Traditionally the Jews have called this future time the "Kingdom of God." It would be a time when God's righteous rule would extend over the whole earth.

Traditional and modern Jews disagree about how it will come and what it will be. Traditional Jews still refer to a Messiah, a person selected by God to bring in the Kingdom, since men have thus far been unable to do it alone. Liberal Jews prefer to think of every man as a messiah, who does whatever he can to advance the cause of righteousness. Gradually, then, the Kingdom will arrive.

The Jewish hope and the Christian hope for a righteous world order are very similar—even though they have been expressed in differing terms. And Jews declare that it is to be universal, for they believe that the righteous of all nations will have a share in the world to come.

The Jews' great interest in living rightly now and in improving the world has lessened their concern about life beyond the grave. Jews do not agree among themselves on this subject. Some traditional Jews have faith in a life beyond the grave that includes punishment and reward, a bodily resurrection, and eternity in Heaven or Hell. More liberal Jews consider none of these beliefs important. Though they believe that the quality of personality (or the soul) cannot die, they do not care to make theories about it. This life, for them, is the life that is important. Doing the right thing now is of more value than believing something. Many Jews feel that repentance and good deeds for one hour in this world are better than the whole life of the world to come.

The Promised Land

The Jews have been the world's best-known displaced persons. More than two thousand years ago, world events left them without a permanent home and sent them forth to roam the earth. Wherever they settled, they kept alive their traditions and their worship of God. Often they stayed together in their own communities, in order that they might better keep their holy days and their dietary laws.

Other people found the Jewish ways different and sometimes difficult to understand. The differences caused some people to complain, and even to persecute the Jews. The Jews have suffered more severe treatment from their neighbors than any other single religious group. Christians particularly—accusing the Jews of having killed Jesus—have been guilty of such persecution. Even today, unscrupulous leaders can find a scapegoat in the Jews, inciting hatred against them. Why the Jews have been so treated is a serious problem that still concerns students of history, sociology, anthropology, and religion.

The isolation forced upon them and the persecution by many neighbors through many years made the Jews more dependent upon one another and upon their traditions than they might otherwise have been. For over two thousand years, they have recalled the ancient promise of God about a land that would be theirs. This was the legendary promised land sought by the Hebrews who left Egypt under the leadership of Moses. This land they had for a time, but they were conquered by one nation after another, only to be driven out in the end.

Many Jews have kept alive the hope that once again the land of Palestine would be theirs. To help bring peace to a land troubled by outbreaks of violence between the most ardent Jewish nationalists, called Zionists, and their ancient enemies, the Arabs, the United Nations in 1948 agreed to a partition of Palestine—Israel for the Jews and Jordan for the Arabs. The arbitrary boundaries could not, of course, completely resolve the age-old hostilities, which were complicated by the fact that both states laid claim to Jerusalem, a city sacred to Islam as well as to Judiasm and Christianity. The United Nations adopted a resolution to internationalize the city but could get support neither from Israel nor from Jordan. The city, then, like the land, remains divided. A further cause for bitterness is that many Jews had to leave their homes on the Jordan side of the border, just as many Arabs had to move from the Israel side when the country was partitioned. There is now between the states a kind of hostile peace; but the tensions go very deep.

Israel has opened its gates to Jews from all over the world. It is yet too early to see what effect this will have on the religion of Judaism, which for long centuries was without a country of its own. Many Jews do not consider the new nation really important to their religion, for they believe that their religious lives can be lived out wherever they now find themselves. Jewish worship does not depend on a national home.

There is no central religious leader in Judaism. Each congregation governs itself. Rabbis are laymen—not priests. They teach the people and try to clarify the Law. They do not speak to God for the people. The people are their own priests; they worship God for themselves.

For a long time, all Jews were "orthodox"—that is, they all followed the laws as listed in their sacred books, to the best of their understanding and ability. But the pressures and changes of modern life made this increasingly difficult. Some came to believe that a modern world view required changes in their personal expression of religious practices. So, in relatively modern times, many Jews have moved away from a strict interpretation of the faith, morality, and practices of their fathers.

Orthodox Judaism. Those who still try to be faithful to the ancient traditions interpreted very strictly are known as "Orthodox" Jews. They consider the whole *Torah* to have been divinely inspired and revealed by God to Moses. They keep all the Mosaic laws, including the dietary restrictions and the strict Sabbath limitations. They use Hebrew in all their synagogue services. Special schools, which they support, teach their children Jewish history and the beginnings of the Hebrew language. Many Orthodox Jews still look for the coming of the personal Messiah.

Conservative Judaism. "Conservative" Jews are those who honor and respect the *Torah*, but who believe in interpreting it through modern Biblical scholarship in order to understand it better. They believe it is important to continue in the traditional forms of worship, with Hebrew used in their services. On the Sabbath they do only necessary work, and they try to make it a day of prayer.

Reform Judaism. A modern American movement has attracted many Jews in this country. It is Reform Judaism and it is a result of an effort to adapt Judaism to twentieth-century Western life. Reform Jews read the *Torah* with an eye to its truth as determined by its agreement with reason and experience. The whole tradition of their people is something they regard with respect. The worship is somewhat similar to that of Protestant Christian churches. Families sit together for services that include organ music and choirs, with the liturgy in Hebrew, but the sermon in English. Both boys and girls are confirmed.

The great teachers of Judaism have made a tremendous contribution to the religious thought of all men. They taught that love of God and of one's fellow man go hand in hand. Life is one, just as God is one. The freedom, dignity, and responsibility of every human being are rooted in the very nature of the universe. Thus it is inevitable, if my own life is to be fulfilled, that I love my neighbor as myself. This follows from loving God "with all thy heart, with all thy soul, and with all thy might."

Jews agree that we cannot know the final answers to the mysteries of life and God. But Jews declare that in the goodness of lives lived righteously, the goodness of God is known:

O Lord, how can we know Thee? Where can we find Thee? Thou art as close to us as breathing and yet art farther than the farthermost star. Thou art as mysterious as the vast solitudes of the night and yet art as familiar to us as the light of the sun. To the seer of old Thou didst say: Thou canst not see my face, but I will make all my goodness pass before thee. Even so does Thy goodness pass before us in the realm of nature and in the varied experiences of our lives. When justice burns like a flaming fire within us, when love evokes willing sacrifice from us, when, to the last full measure of selfless devotion, we proclaim our belief in the ultimate triumph of truth and righteousness, do we not bow before the vision of Thy goodness? Thou livest within our hearts, as Thou dost pervade the world, and we through righteousness behold Thy presence.

14. Festivals and Holy Days

THE JEWS have always treasured their traditions. Many of their most meaningful religious and family customs center about their festivals and holy days.

The Sabbath

At sunset on Friday evening, candles are lighted in millions of Jewish homes all over the world. This is a sign to the assembled family that the Sabbath has begun, bringing twenty-four hours of worship and rest. When the fathers and older sons return from the service at the synagogue, there are special family rites of blessing and prayer. Then all sit down to the best and happiest meal of the week, frequently sharing it with some visitor invited home after the synagogue service.

The next morning the whole family attends a worship service in the synagogue, the men and boys sitting in the assembly hall, and the women and girls going to the women's gallery. The service itself varies with the congregation. Usually it includes the chanting of portions of the Torah and the Psalms led by the cantor, a Jewish layman who is skilled at this work. There are times for many prayers and readings from the Torah. There may also be a sermon given by the rabbi.

Upon returning home, Jews rest in the manner which pleases each, although Orthodox Jews have many restrictions upon work, play, and travel. In the afternoon, some men and boys return to the synagogue for a period of reading and discussion. Orthodox Jews have planned for the day so carefully that the cooking and cleaning have been accomplished before the Sabbath. Conservative Jews do only necessary work, and Reform Jews observe the day as one of rest and worship, with no particular limitations on their activities. At nightfall, the family gathers again to note the end of the Sabbath and the beginning of a new week.

For countless years, the Sabbath has been the distinctive

center of Jewish home life. This age-old custom of observing one day out of seven for rest and formal worship was a great contribution that the Jews made to the world. It has for long been shared by Christians and Moslems—though different days have been chosen for the purpose.

In the beginning, the Jewish Sabbath was a new ideal to masses of people who toiled long hours day after day, with no weekends or vacations. Jews are asked to "observe the Sabbath and keep it holy," for everyone needs such rest and change. It is probable that this regular weekly plan of alternation between rest and activity, between work and worship, contributed greatly to the success of Jews in many fields.

In the Ten Commandments, Jews are reminded of God's example: ". . . . in six days the Lord made the heavens, the earth, and the sea, together with all that is in them, but rested on the seventh day: that is how the Lord came to bless the seventh day and to hallow it." This adds the emphasis of religion to the need for rest. Wise rabbis have taught that the Sabbath must minister to man's need as well as to God. For the Jews, human life has always been of greater concern than an abstract rule.

Rosh Hashonah: The New Year

In the seventh month of the Jewish calendar, Jews are called to a long period of thought and penitence. The beginning of the New Year is observed solemnly in the synagogues with the blowing of a ram's horn, called the shofar. This sound opens a ten-day season for Jews to take stock of their lives and seek forgiveness for their shortcomings.

Since the Jewish calendar is based on the cycle of the moon rather than the sun, the exact date varies from year to year. Rosh Hashonah may come early in September or early in October.

To most Jews, the ten-day period is a time of judgment. An ancient tradition states that during this period God determines who shall live and who shall die; who shall be at rest and who shall wander; who shall be tranquil and who shall be harassed; who shall become poor and who shall wax rich; who shall be brought low and who shall be exalted. The old traditions further say that Rosh Hashonah is the day on which God writes in the great Book of Judgment the record of everyone's life.

The ten days that follow allow time for a person to think through his life and what he can do about it. They allow him time and opportunity to see his mistakes and try to correct them. They are solemn, holy days. Traditional Jews believe that a person may even have his record in the Book of Judgment changed, if he is sincere, kind, and penitent enough. They believe that the Book of Judgment is closed again at the end of the ten days.

The climax of the new year observance is Yom Kippur, the tenth day of the new year. It begins at sundown (as do all Jewish holy days) and continues for twenty-four hours. Traditionally, adult Jews neither eat nor drink during this day. They spend their time in thought and prayer. There is a solemn service in the synagogue, which every Jew tries to attend. It opens with a haunting melody, the Kol Nidre chant. This is a plea for release from religious vows that could not be kept—a reference to the persecutions which Jews have suffered again and again at the hands of non-Jews. The close of the Yom Kippur service is again the sound of the ram's horn. It signifies the closing of the Book of Judgment until the following year.

The ideas of the Book of Judgment and God as the Great Judge are found in other religions too. And Jews, like others, may interpret the traditions literally. Or they may interpret them in a profoundly personal and spiritual sense. These "Days of Awe," as they are sometimes called, are days for a Jew to ask important questions about life and to continue his spiritual growth. Judaism does not offer believers easy answers to their religious questions. Instead, it encourages them to search their hearts and lives for better ways of living.

Jews are not taught that mankind is basically sinful or that normal needs and interests are wrong. There are no monks or nuns in Judaism. Instead, Jews emphasize the great beauty of family life. During the new year observance, Jews are encouraged to think about their relationships with other people. Have they acted with true love and justice? Have they been humble, remembering their limitations? Are they in need of forgiveness for sins committed against their fellow men?

Acts of loving-kindness are the best means of making amends. As the rabbis have said: "Whoever has a sin to confess and is ashamed to do so, let him go and do a good deed and he will find forgiveness."

During the *Yom Kippur* service, some verses are read from the book of *Isaiah*. They point out to the worshiping Jew that the heart of religion is loving concern for others:

Is not this the fast that I have chosen?
To loose the bands of wickedness,
To undo the heavy burdens,
And to let the oppressed go free . . . ?
Is it not to deal thy bread to the hungry,
And that thou bring the poor that are cast out to thy
house?
When thou seest the naked, that thou cover him;
And that thou hide not thyself from thine own flesh?
Then shall thy light break forth as the morning . . .
And thy righteousness shall go before thee.

Succos: The Feast of Tabernacles

One of the most joyful Jewish holy days is the celebration of *Succos*, which comes at the time of harvest, when the vines are heavy with grapes and the grain stands ripe in the fields. It is a festival of thanksgiving, lasting for nine days. It reminds Jews of the time of the Exodus of the Jewish people from Egypt, when they were forced to live in small shelters (called *succos*) along the way. Jews often make replicas of these shelters, which are also called tabernacles. They decorate them with flowers, fruits and branches as reminders of the generosity of God.

Modern Jews think of the often sorrowful history of their fellow believers, as well as about other people. On the Sabbath during *Succos*, this prayer is recited:

We recall today with grateful hearts Thy loving providence which guided our fathers in their wanderings through the barren desert and the trackless wilderness. . . . We thank Thee that the same unfailing mercies have guided and sheltered us, their children, in all the years of our pilgrimage. . . . We pray Thee that the enjoyment of Thy blessings may awaken within us a spirit of contentment and fortitude, that we may neither grow proud through success nor become embittered by failure.

May we sympathize with those whose hopes have been disappointed and whose labors have been unfruitful. May our hands be outstretched to those who suffer, and our hearts be open to those who are in need. Praised be Thou, O Lord, Giver of all good. Amen.

On the ninth day of the *Succos* celebration, there is a joyful ceremony in the synagogue, when the scrolls of the *Torah* are carried about in a gay procession. Sometimes there are dances and songs in which all join. This is one more way in which Jews show their love for the *Torah*. On this day, the last verses of the *Torah* (Deuteronomy 34) are read. Then the rabbi turns back to the first verse of Genesis: "In the beginning, God . . ." This begins the annual reading of the whole *Torah* in each synagogue.

Hanukkah: Feast of Dedication

The celebration of *Hanukkah* is a feast of dedication that usually comes in December. Jews observe it for eight days, during which there are special services in the synagogues, special holiday foods, and gifts. *Hanukkah* recalls to modern Jews a significant event in the past, when their ancestors fought for religious freedom.

In the second century B.C., the Syrians had gained control of Palestine, and they were trying to force the Jews to discontinue their religion. Some of the Jews did as they were commanded. Others refused, despite Syrian reprisals. An elderly priest, Mattathias, began a revolt. Later his son, Judah Maccabee, carried the revolt much farther and won final victory over the Syrian army. In celebration of their regained freedom, the Jews went to Jerusalem to cleanse the temple and renew Jewish worship there. They found a single unopened container of the oil used in their services. According to tradition it burned before the altar for eight days.

Now Jews burn eight candles during *Hanukkah*, often lighting one the first evening, two the second, and so on. They often call *Hanukkah* the Festival of Lights. *Hanukkah* is a time of great rejoicing and a time of solemn reminder of how precious liberty is. Jews especially are thankful at this time for the freedom to worship according to their own consciences. The struggle for freedom of thought and worship is never finished completely. It is an ongoing task. Jews recognize this as they pray a special Sabbath prayer during *Hanukkah*:

Bless, O God, the Chanukah [*Hanukkah*] lights, that they may shed their radiance into our homes and our lives. May they kindle within us the flame of faith and zeal that, like the Maccabees of old, we battle bravely for Thy cause. Make us ever worthy of Thy love and Thy blessing, our Shield and Protector. Amen.

Purim

In the early spring—usually in March—Jews celebrate a particularly joyful holy day. In the synagogues, the people assemble to hear the reading of the *Megillah*, the *Book of Esther*. In contrast to their usually serious attention in services, the Jews on this day distribute noisemakers among the children, for use at certain places in the reading. Later the children may dramatize the ancient story. Friends and relatives often exchange gifts, and many Jews enjoy a special cookie, called a Haman tart.

The story that they hear in the synagogue concerns a beautiful Jewish woman of long ago, Esther, the wife of the king of Persia. Esther's uncle, Mordecai, happened to arouse the hatred of a high court official named Haman. For revenge, Haman began a plan to exterminate all the Jews, accusing them unjustly of disloyalty to the king. When Esther learned of the plan, she risked death to expose Haman's schemes, revealing her own Jewishness to the king. As a result, the king honored Mordecai—and Haman died on the gallows that he himself had prepared for Mordecai.

Jews enjoy hearing the annual reading of the story. They enjoy the carnival atmosphere that pervades the synagogue on this night, with the children vigorously using the noisemakers whenever Haman's name is mentioned. They do not concern themselves very much with whether or not the story is true as it is read. Many Jewish scholars claim that it is simply an historical novel.

However, the meaning of the story is real and true. It is a tale of hatred directed at Jews simply because of their Jewishness. Haman's chief charge against the Jews was that their ways were "different." This charge and others like it have been hurled against the Jews countless times in the past. It is no wonder that they have made an annual celebration of this story of the downfall of one anti-Jewish oppressor.

Jews celebrate *Purim* not only for this reason, but also in recognition of common brotherhood. Many rabbis say that the basic idea to this day is that differences among men do not need to cause dissension. Deeper than all differences is our humanity. In the story, the king's acceptance of the people whose ways were different shows that he saw the shared humanity under the outward diversity.

The Passover

The Jews, like all people, have a celebration in the springtime. Long ago, people celebrated the renewed fertility of the earth, the newborn animals among their flocks, and the new growth of plant life. For many hundreds of years, Jews have held a spring festival to commemorate the legendary events described in the first chapters of the book of Exodus.

For many years the Jews had been held in what amounted to slavery in Egypt. Moses became their spokesman, and he sought their release from the Egyptian Pharaoh. But this ruler became quite stubborn, according to the legends, despite the several plagues that God had sent against the Egyptians. So God sent an angel of death to kill all the first-born in the land of Egypt, both of men and flocks. The Israelites, however, were spared. They had marked their houses with the blood of a lamb. So the angel of death "passed over" them. The Pharaoh relented, and the Israelites left in great haste. They did not even have time to leaven their bread. It had to be baked unleavened.

During the celebration of the Passover, all leaven is removed from the traditional Jewish home for eight days. The Jews eat matzos, an unleavened bread, to remind them of the sufferings of their ancestors. Sometimes they call the Passover the "Feast of Unleavened Bread." The special bread, certain bitter herbs, and other symbolic foods help them to celebrate the delivery of the Jewish people from bondage.

Many Jews have never taken the story of the plagues and miracles in the book of Exodus as being literally and historically true. This is a matter for personal or critical interpretation of the texts of their scriptures. Some of the rabbis have taught that the "plague of darkness," for example, was simply another name for superstition and spiritual blindness. Therefore, some Jews celebrate the Passover not only as freedom from an oppressive tyrant but as freedom from bondage to evil habits or intentions.

Jewish holidays do not celebrate simply and solely things that are supposed to have happened in the past. The holidays always have a significant meaning for the present. This is because Jewish customs are inwardly experienced by Jews—not garments put on for occasions. Just so, on the Passover, while Jews think about the bondage of long ago, they also pray for enslaved people of today:

> God of freedom, Thy children still groan under the burden of cruel taskmasters. Slavery debases their bodies and minds, and robs them of the enjoyment of Thy bounties. The fear of cruelty and the peril of death blight the souls of men. O break Thou the irons that bind them. Teach men to understand that by forging chains for others they forge chains for themselves, that as long as some are in fetters no one is truly free. Help them to see that liberty is the very breath of life and that only in the atmosphere of freedom can truth, prosperity and peace flourish.

Shavuos

Ancient Jews celebrated this festival at the time of the barley harvest in Palestine. Later, Jews held the festival of *Shavuos* to commemorate God's giving the *Torah* to Moses. Their keeping of this festival stresses their underlying religious faith that the universe has law, order, and purpose.

In synagogue services, the *Book of Ruth* is read to the congregation. In Reform and Conservative synagogues, this occasion includes the confirmation of children. Children who have completed a course of study under the rabbi's instruction declare before the congregation their loyalty to God and their intention of living by his laws.

In these ways the Jews face life's demands and mysteries, firm in their belief in God and proud of their traditions. For thousands of years, no matter what they have faced, Jews have gained assurance from the Law of the Lord. They have gained strength from their simple declaration: "The Lord is One."

CHRISTIANITY

15. Jesus and the Kingdom of God

THE PLACE of Jesus in history is not solely that of an individual of two thousand years ago. Jesus is a religious symbol. The facts of his life have been embroidered with the hopes and dreams of generations of Christians. For these reasons it is almost impossible to get a true historical picture of the man who unintentionally became the founder of the Christian religion, and even—to many Christians—God himself.

We should approach the study of Jesus in the same way that we approach the study of other religious prophets and leaders. We need respect, frankness, and an open mind. It is well to remember that the tendency to glorify or even deify a great religious leader has characterized the growth of most religions. The history of Christian attitudes illustrates this—as do the histories of Taoism and Buddhism. Intent on exalting the divine role that the Church has given to Jesus, many have missed finding the wisdom of his teachings. They have worshiped him—but failed to follow him. Yet the Jesus whom some at least can see behind all the adoration sought not to make men accept *himself*, but to accept his way of life. And what was this way?

Stories of Jesus

We have no written records from the time when Jesus lived. The oldest stories about him that we can find are included in the Christian New Testament. The Gospel According to Mark is usually considered to be the earliest of these. Yet it was written over forty years after the death of Jesus. It is interesting to notice that it is the simplest of the Gospels. Years later, other Gospels were written—Matthew, Luke, and John. Each of them was written for a purpose: to present Jesus and his work in a way that would appeal to a new group of people.

Some parts of these *Gospels* are similar, but there are a good many differences. For example, the *Gospel* writers do not agree on the baptism of Jesus or the religious experience that led to his baptism and to his teaching. They do not agree as to the existence of signs from God to prove to everyone that Jesus was his unique son.

The writers disagree—and so do Christian scholars today —on Jesus' belief about the Kingdom of God. Some say that Jesus, like many of the Jews in the Palestine of his day, expected it to come in dramatic, world-shaking fashion. Others say that he thought of it solely as an inner Kingdom which would emerge slowly in the hearts of people. There are *New Testament* passages that support each interpretation. There are passages that declare Jesus' expectation of an important role in the Kingdom, as a representative of God. And there are other passages that present him more as a humble teacher like Amos, Hosea, or the other prophets.

Because of such interesting differences in interpretation of details, scholars recognize that we can never know Jesus as he really was. We can know him only as he was remembered by the children and grandchildren of those who first heard and knew him. The historian knows that this is a problem common to all religions, but Christians have made more attempts to "prove" things by appealing to their scriptures than many other people have. Such "proof" has not been of great concern to Buddhists and Hindus, for example. They believe that truth is timeless. It is as available to each person through his own experience as it is to important religious leaders.

Thus we should know at the beginning that there is little we can prove about the way that Jesus lived and taught. Where honest scholars disagree, it is important that we read the records for ourselves. In that way we may become aware of the difficult problems involved in choosing any interpretation. Each of us must remember that without real effort he will find in the records only what he wishes to discover there. Too often what we find tells more about our own personalities than it does about the truth we seek.

The story of Jesus is not ended with his death. It stretches into the centuries of Christianity. Jesus committed himself to the will of God, as he understood it, and to the urgent requirements of the Kingdom of God. This commitment and the drama of his life have made Jesus a directing factor in the lives of Christians. More than nineteen centuries have passed since he spoke to disciples and followers. Let us strip back the layers of years to discover, as best we can, how he taught and lived.

John the Baptizer

On an ordinary day in Palestine in about the year 26 A.D., a man called John the Baptizer was teaching close by the banks of the River Jordan. His fame as a fiery, stern teacher had already spread about the countryside. And on this day there were many people who had walked long distances to hear him. Once there, they sat on the hard stones in the parching heat.

They were so held by the speaker that they did not notice the discomforts of this arid section of Judea. John spoke to them urgently and sternly. He preached of a new kind of life that they must live—a life marked by repentance for their past wrongdoings. They must repent now, for the Kingdom of God was about to come, bringing with it peace and satisfaction for the righteous, but dreadful suffering for sinners. The comforts of life, offerings in the Temple, rituals and ceremonies of worship—these did not matter. What did matter was a radical change of life, with one's whole being cleansed and righted by repentance.

Among those who listened most attentively to John's insistent words that afternoon was a young man named Jesus. Jesus had come all the way from Nazareth to hear this new teacher, who lived as a hermit in the wilderness but drew crowds even there through the force of his message. Jesus was strangely stirred by the words he heard, by their boldness, their sincerity, and their power. He watched as others accepted John's invitation to go down into the River Jordan to be baptized as a sign of their repentance and their promises to live new lives. After a time of listening, Jesus too went down to be baptized by John.

A New Decision

Jesus was profoundly moved by this experience. He seemed to feel that God took notice of his action and was pleased with it. Not long after this, Jesus went away into the wilderness by himself to think through what his life should be thereafter. In the time of his solitary thought,

Jesus became convinced that God wanted him to live his life in a special way, teaching others and helping them.

Yet Jesus felt that he did not want to be the same kind of teacher as John, living away from people in the rough and lonely wilds. Instead, Jesus would carry his message to the people in the towns and cities, as well as those in the countryside. He was filled with a great desire to teach those who faced the everyday problems of life and religion —not just those who were able to leave homes and daily comforts, as John's followers had. He went home to tell his family and friends what he had decided to do.

It was not easy to carry out his decision. Most people among his family and friends could not understand or appreciate his intentions. To some of them, Jesus had always seemed to be very serious, but they had never expected to see him depart so radically from the usual kind of life. His mother, his brothers, and his sisters had come to depend upon him for their livelihood, since the death of his father, Joseph. How could they get along without him?

He had to face the objections and perhaps the ridicule of the people of his village. Some of them would have approved of his leaving had he been going to join one of the many anti-Roman underground movements. But how was he going to help his people overcome their conquerors merely by becoming a wandering preacher? Possibly, also, Jesus had to face lingering doubts about whether he could actually live in the way he planned. There would be no home, no income, and no friends upon whom he could depend. All that he ever ate or wore would have to be provided by those who listened to what he told them. Would what he taught them be worth what they gave?

Despite all arguments, he went ahead. He had expected such difficulties. What strength he needed to carry out his plans came from the inspiration that had led to them. Alone and lacking the approval of relatives and friends, he set off for Capernaum, to begin there the ministry that led to his death and to the birth of the Christian religion. ·

God and His Kingdom

Jesus' decision, like most such decisions, had deep roots. As a child, Jesus had learned the Jewish history and scriptures from his father and from synagogue leaders. He knew well the ever-present Jewish hope for a brighter, better future, when God would help the Jews to regain their freedom and prestige among the nations. This hope flamed high in their hearts, as they lived under Roman conquerors.

For some time Jesus had thought carefully about this national hope, and he now knew that he could not fully agree with those who held it. Many of the Jews had gotten into a hopeless feeling that what they as individuals did was not important. They believed that sometime God was going to cause a miracle, bringing into being a new age, when Palestine would be powerful, independent, and respected among the nations. There would be no occupying armies or foreign governors. The Jewish people would live in the same prosperous way they had lived under King David of long ago. To inaugurate this new age, God's anointed one, the Messiah, would overcome their enemies. Then he would rule in the Kingdom of God, for which generations of Jews had hoped.

This could not be the way in which God would bring a thing to pass, Jesus had decided. God did not send his blessings to some and withhold them from others. God's blessings came to a person in the quiet, transforming knowledge that his life was the best he could live. The Kingdom of God was not a condition that waited in some undisclosed future. No, the Kingdom of God was a present possibility of goodness that was hidden, like a seed, inside every person. You have only to let it grow naturally, aiding its development by loving attitudes and kind deeds. And behold, it grows gradually until you yourself are part of the Kingdom of God.

Jesus' ideas about the Kingdom stemmed very naturally from his beliefs about God. Jesus had had the kind of religious training that all loyal Jews tried to give their children. He had heard the stories of the prophets. He knew many of the Psalms, which described God's love and mercy. Most important of all, Jesus had taken the time to develop a close personal relationship with his God. Prayer and meditation had led him to feel at home with God. Later, Jesus was to tell many parables describing God as like a father, forgiving, concerned, and loving. Throughout his life, he was to turn to God as to a guide, a source of strength and inspiration, ever available to the call of meditation and prayer.

Often Jesus was to refer to the will of God when he taught and comforted his hearers. God expected something of men, to be sure. He expected them to behave toward each other with loving concern, forgiveness, and patience, just as he dealt with them. This was the righteousness God's Kingdom required, not a righteousness bound up with many rules and practices. This righteousness went much deeper—as deep as the thoughts and intentions and desires. From these roots it flowed out into righteous speech, righteous acts, and righteous efforts.

Jesus and His Teachings

In Capernaum and in most of the towns to which he later went, Jesus was well received by the common people. He came to them with a special message of hope. Many of them could not afford the special sacrifices that had to be taken annually to the temple at Jerusalem. The priests had told them that such sacrifices must be offered if they wished to be in God's favor. What were they to do? Jesus said that the offerings of a contrite heart and a pure life were far more important to God than offerings of first fruits or year-old kids.

Some of the people who listened gladly to Jesus were those who felt extremely guilty for rules they had not kept. There were countless Jewish laws telling them what to eat and how it should be served and prescribing the observance of many small religious customs. The poor people who spent all their time eking out their meager existence had no opportunity and often no information about such rules. Many of the Jewish priests and teachers condemned them as sinners. Jesus told the people that they should not be so concerned with the outward performance of the laws that they forgot the spirit of the laws. The laws and the prophets of his people's religion had emphasized two things: love of God and love of neighbor.

Some people had become ill because they were so filled with feelings of sinfulness or so upset by their constant failure to do all that their religion required. To people like these, Jesus' message was like medicine. They were sick at heart, and that had made some of them ill. His words and his understanding made them feel better, and their health returned. Through such situations, Jesus gained a reputation as a healer. Many people were attracted to him for this reason. Sometimes he became discouraged that there were so many people who wanted to be healed, but so few who wanted to join him in living by the will of God.

Not all of the people liked what they heard. There were many Jews who felt that a man could not possibly live a good life unless he fulfilled each Jewish law in the most exacting detail. They did not like to hear anyone say that laws were not important. Some of the religious leaders became very angry as Jesus' reputation as a healer increased. They thought that sinful people deserved to suffer. What right did Jesus have to make them feel that they had been forgiven? God alone knew whether they were forgiven.

Other Jews were troubled because Jesus seemed to be too peaceful and too loving. He did not even hate their enemies, the occupying Roman soldiers. They knew the history of their race, with all its humiliating defeats and invasions. This Roman occupation was only one of a long chain of occupations by conquerors. Some of Jesus' followers had hoped that he might prove himself to be the forceful Messiah, who was to come to help them attain a position of power and prosperity once again. When he continued to teach love and patience, some of them gave up in disgust. Some kept on following, still hoping that he would be such a Messiah in the end.

A good many followers could not understand what it was that Jesus was saying when he described his ideas of the Kingdom of God. He emphasized again and again that people did not have to wait until conditions were ideal in order to live in the right way. A man is what he is inside himself.

This quality of the inner life is not determined by occupying armies, by exact following of laws, or by large offerings at the Temple. The thought you have before you speak is more important than what you say. The attitude you have underneath your act is more important than what you do.

Jesus told beautiful stories to make the Kingdom seem real to his listeners. The Kingdom of God is like a mustard seed, smallest of all the seeds. But when it is grown, the mustard plant is very large. Just so, the Kingdom within is at first so tiny that one may not even be aware of it. But when it is fully developed, it overshadows everything else in a person's life. The Kingdom of God is like a treasure hidden in a field. When a man discovered it, he rushed out and sold everything he had in order to buy that field. In the same way, when a man discovers the inestimable value of the Kingdom, he gives up everything for it.

To Jesus, the Kingdom of God was the ultimate goal of all human effort. There was really nothing else worth seeking. Men were designed to live in such a Kingdom. It did not depend upon a certain time or a certain place. The Kingdom of God required only righteous people as its citizens, only mercy, kindness, and love as its laws. Wherever there were righteous people using mercy, kindness, and love as their way of life, there was the Kingdom of God.

When Jesus spoke of the Kingdom of God, he was filled with a sense of urgency. People must not fold their hands and wait for God to bring in the Kingdom. The time was now. People must discover their capacity for goodness and begin to live in the right way. Jesus told people that this required repentance. They must leave their old ways of living behind and henceforth choose and live righteously, by the will of God. Then the Kingdom of God would come. God was ready. Men must be, too.

Since he felt so strongly that every person must meet the conditions of the Kingdom, Jesus took his message to many so-called sinful people. Those who criticized him found it easy to point to occasions when he had talked with the hated tax-collectors or visited with persons of questionable reputation. How could a man be a good religious teacher if he kept such poor company? Jesus answered, "I came not to call the righteous, but sinners to repentance."

Over and over Jesus repeated that God did not blame sinners half so much as some people did. God is ready with forgiveness the moment a person sincerely asks for it. God is like a father who sees his son leave home, bent upon wasting his money and his time in a foolish search for pleasure. The moment the son returns, sadder and wiser, and determined to live rightly, the father welcomes him eagerly, forgetting his blame for the joy of having him again. Even so, the Father in Heaven welcomes those who are so sorry for past foolishness that they are sincerely ready to try to live by His will.

Friends and Enemies

At the end of a year or so of teaching, Jesus had collected a number of followers. Twelve of them, later known as the disciples, had been so impressed with their master's message that they, too, had given up homes and families and occupations. Like Jesus, they felt that the demands of the Kingdom blotted out all lesser considerations. Everything else was secondary to life's spiritual search.

Jesus became increasingly aware that his activities were meeting with disapproval from many sources. The officials of the Jewish religion, who had never been enthusiastic about his mission, became more hostile. The Romans, who wished mainly for peace and order, suspected any radical movement of having revolutionary plans. They began to fear Jesus' talk of the coming Kingdom, even though to Jesus it was completely spiritual.

For a long time, there had been warnings that the way of life he had chosen might lead to his death. There would have been time to change his teachings so that he would not incur the wrath of the powerful priests. There would have been time to reassure the Romans by speaking less emphatically of the Kingdom of God. Such compromises were impossible for Jesus, in the light of his central concern with the will of God. He might have stayed away from Jerusalem, but this was the center of Judaism. He felt he had a message to give and a part to take in the Passover celebration. He had always joined in the religious feasts of his people. So, at the height of the holiday excitement, Jesus and his disciples entered Jerusalem.

His Ministry Ends

During this visit, Jesus was put to death on the cross, at the hands of the Romans. Probably some of the priests or some of the zealous Jewish patriots had helped to convince them that this man was a rabble-rouser who worked against the welfare of the state. Some of the patriots were disappointed that Jesus still refused to lead a revolt against Rome. The priests could feel more secure in their positions after he was gone. There were no masses of people to cry out in Jesus' behalf. The large numbers of followers had left him before that, discouraged with the fruitless waiting for him to declare himself to be the Messiah. It seemed to some of his disciples that the whole religious adventure had begun to demand too much. They abandoned Jesus in fear for their own safety.

Jesus must have had many moments of discouragement in his last days. He had seen people who wished him to do things his convictions would not let him do. He had seen his disciples acting in ways that showed they still did not fully understand what he had tried so long to teach them about the will of God. He had known for some time that he might be killed. Was his death to come before he accomplished all he had set out to do? Was he to leave his people still unprepared to be the avenues through which God would work to bring in the Kingdom? How hard it must have been to see his efforts ended before he had reached his goals.

Christianity Begins

But the end had come. The bewildered disciples went into hiding. Later, when they felt safe, they met together and talked in hushed tones of the tragic thing that had happened. Their sorrow led them into deeper fellowship, and they recalled together the experiences they had shared with Jesus. From this early fellowship, Christianity began.

In many ways, Christianity differs greatly from the simple religion of Jesus. But for the chief ideas of its faith, it looks back to the humble, dedicated young man from Galilee, who said that a man must commit himself wholly to God, and then to his neighbor. Jesus' death, as a consequence of his beliefs, was the next logical step in his own life of consecration to the task of bringing the Kingdom of God on earth.

16. Foundations of the Faith

I T IS EASY to understand the bewilderment and fear of those early followers of Jesus who witnessed his arrest and his crucifixion. He was killed as a criminal, and they, having shared in his work, feared that they must surely share in his punishment. With great haste they hid, and for a time the movement seemed no longer to exist.

When the danger had passed and the disciples of Jesus had begun to see each other again, they recalled the joys and sorrows of their days spent with the Master. Together they looked for comfort for their grief in telling and retelling stories of Jesus. So constantly did they live with his memory that Jesus seemed still with them. Some began to believe that he was not dead. True, he had died upon the cross and had been buried. But now he lived again. He had left them only briefly, to prepare for ushering in the new age, the Kingdom of God.

The First Christians

These convictions came easily to the first-century Christians. They were men of their time, whose ignorance often held them to superstitious beliefs. Sometimes they believed literally in their dreams and visions. They believed in demons and angels. They believed that dead bodies could sometimes come out of graves. Now they believed that Jesus would return.

To nourish their hope, they recalled statements they thought Jesus had made. Had he not announced that the Kingdom was coming almost immediately? Had he not called them from their ordinary lives to work with him for its coming? Had he not promised that they could share in it? Surely it was so. He would come again, and the Kingdom of God would come with him. He was, after all, the Messiah!

Afire with the urgency of their message, the disciples rushed to tell others. Jesus would be back soon to bring in the Kingdom of God. This would happen within their generation! Numbers of Jews heard and heeded the warning to prepare themselves. Later, when year after year passed and nothing happened, the urgency of the message began to be spent.

Christianity Leaves Judaism

Jesus' teachings were never to become a part of his native Jewish religion. Jesus had directed his message to those who had not found comfort in strict Judaism. Many followers were drawn from the fringes of Jewish life, both in religion and in politics. Strengthened by the influence of Jesus, these people moved farther than ever from the more orthodox Jesus. Even so, it was a long time before the Jewish-Christians would admit Gentiles (non-Jews) into their fellowship.

The disciple Peter was among those who insisted upon keeping the movement exclusively Jewish. But later, when Paul became a Christian, he persuaded Peter and others to admit Gentiles into the group. After that, it was not long before non-Jews outnumbered Jews in the Christian movement.

Jesus as the Christ of Christianity

Of all the people associated with the beginnings of Christianity, Paul was most responsible for the turn its beliefs took. He added a new note that determined its future course. The new idea came from the popular "mystery cult" religions that abounded in the Mediterranean lands. The "mystery" applied to a mystical, symbolic union with a god who lived in human form, died, but came to life again. Through a secret ceremony that symbolically united him with his god, the believer was assured that he could change his human nature to divine nature and thus gain a happy afterlife. There were a number of mystery cults, with different gods. But all of them emphasized the salvation resulting from dedication to a dying-rising Lord.

It is interesting that the word *Kyrios* (Lord), which the Greeks applied to the dying-rising god, was used by Paul to apply to Jesus. It was natural that those who heard Jesus called *Kyrios* should interpret him in a mystery-cult sense. For many converts to Christianity, Jesus was from the first a savior-god in a human body.

One of the greatest debates in Christian history was about whether Jesus was a god, like God, or the God. After a great deal of angry oratory, it was finally decided that Jesus was "very God of very God." This debate was only one of many theological wrangles, most of which would not have developed had Jesus lived long enough to help organize a new and growing religion. As it was, Jesus probably would not have been interested anyway. Life, to him, was not something to be argued and debated. Neither was religion. A man must live religion, not debate it.

Christians have said that Jesus is a personal savior. Usually, they call him the Christ, which means Deliverer or Messiah. They say that Jesus Christ is the Son of God. Most Christians have believed that he shares in God's divinity, that he *is* God himself. He lived and died as a man and for men. But he arose from the grave and ascended into heaven to "sit at the right hand of God," as one famous creed declares.

These definitions developed from the mystery-cult ideas, which are so ancient that most modern Christians do not know of their origin or the reasons for their existence. The ideas have lived long beyond their sources, because they have been included in the creeds of the orthodox Christian churches. There is an old Christian story which tells about the ancient ideas. It is called by many the "story of salvation." It describes men as having been steeped in sinfulness, from the time of the very first people. Men were so filled with wickedness that they no longer knew about goodness. Only God could do anything to redeem them from the situation. So God chose the Hebrew-Jewish people to teach men to rise above their continuing sinfulness.

The Jews did not play their proper part in the plan. So God sent Jesus Christ, his only Son, to bring men back into harmony with himself. Through his life, death, resurrection, and subsequent ascension into Heaven, Jesus did everything that was needed. Through this one divine sacrifice, men could obtain cancellation or forgiveness for their vast sins against God.

Practically all Christians accept the central items in the great dramatic tale as being true, although some do not look upon the words as telling what actually happened. Some feel that it is a way of picturing something that is true. They have said that the story means that people were originally intended to be complete and in right relationship to God.

However, person after person, in generation after generation, made improper choices. They lost the right relationship, and thus they lost the ability to live perfectly. Each person must go through the difficult but rewarding process of finding it again. At the same time that a man is honestly trying, God is interested in his welfare. God has made it possible for a man to find himself again.

By far the majority of Christians have said that Jesus was an essential part of God's way of making salvation possible. This has led Christians to pray to the Christ and to worship him, just as they worship God. In Jesus Christ, many Christians have found all the god they know.

All Christians claim that their beliefs stem from something that Jesus said or did, even though Christians of all sects believe many things of which Jesus himself never heard or spoke. Throughout the development of Christianity, Christians have faced the same universal questions of the nature of man and the nature of God. Most Christians have found answers to these questions that differ greatly from Jesus' own answers. Answers depend upon personal experience. So Christian answers have varied with times and places. But the questions about which people have wondered, in Jesus' day and in our own, are very similar, because men are basically alike.

What Am I?

Christians generally would say that a man is more than what he appears to be. That which is visible, the body, actually is the house of an invisible self. Traditionally, Christians have called this inner self the "soul." A human body is a temporary thing, which finally dies. Its elements blend once more with the elements of the earth. But a human soul is eternal, surviving the death of the body, say most Christians.

The human soul is akin to God in this sense. God is the eternal spirit, existing from before creation. Human souls are created by God, and once created, they also are eternal. Christians believe that each soul is individual, having been united with an individual body since before the person's birth. Through the union of soul and body, a person is brought into being.

Christians have tried to describe the soul in various ways. Some have thought it might be connected with the intelligence, or with the life-force, or with something else. But Christians as a whole have never been able to agree on another word for it. They say "soul," and they mean that it is "that eternal something" which is not some thing. It is not affected by death or other destructive forces. It is that which underlies a man's whole conscious life. It cannot be seen. It occupies no space. It is timeless and changeless. Its existence cannot be proved. It is taken "on faith."

What Is God?

A newborn baby does not know himself to be a person. He must gradually experience the fact that he is someone different from his mother, and then from all those other people he comes to know. He must learn to be conscious of himself. Then he becomes conscious of more and more people with whom he comes into contact.

As he grows and matures in his relationships with himself and with others, he becomes ready for larger experiences. The orderly and changeless laws of nature, which he has observed since childhood; the hopes and needs he shares with his fellows; the dependable cycle of growth and decay, in which he sees all things and beings participate—these are gradually making him conscious of something beyond himself and those like himself. There seems to be a meaning and a plan to life. What is it? What is back of it all?

Such questions have been among the most universal of human wonderings. They have led most people to suggest that something or someone they call God is back of it all. Christians have offered many descriptions of God, even though they admit that God is beyond human understanding and description. He is unlimited in power, in wisdom, in mercy, and in love. He is boundless, invisible, and gracious. He is Judge, Lord, Father.

What these descriptions mean to a person depends entirely on his own experience. Any one of the terms cannot be equally valuable to all. Such descriptions have been like sign posts or pointers along the way. But they have not been as final as some theologians have claimed. It is helpful to remember that when Jesus wanted to pass on something of his own faith and philosophy, he used parables, stories, and poetic figures of speech.

The pages of Christian history reveal many leaders who did not know as much about people as Jesus did. He knew that there is no real understanding apart from experience, either direct or indirect. A person must know and define God for himself. But Christian history contains tales of compulsory beliefs. There have been times when the faith was defined and all who could not accept it were forced to leave the church. There were arguments and wars and persecution, in the name of one creed or another.

Yet always, even at the height of persecution and compulsion, there were some thoughtful people who knew that faith is personal. Creeds cannot really be enforced. One's idea of God is as individual as one's response to a symphony. I cannot possibly hear the symphony for you, nor can I experience God for you. Then why must we describe them in the same terms?

What Is the Holy Spirit?

The Christian story of salvation tells that God revealed his great love when he sent his son among men to be a guide and savior. But Jesus is no longer here to lead people into better ways of living. In his place, says the old story, God sent the Holy Spirit. For many years, great arguments were held in orthodox circles as to the place and function of the Holy Spirit. Most modern Christians are no longer concerned with such debates. The Holy Spirit is looked upon as God is another form. It is the power of God working in and through the life of the believer to sustain him and to keep him in right relationship to God and to his neighbor.

Christianity, then, has three gods or it has one—depending upon the opinions of the person who is doing the explaining. Christians are usually indignant when someone says that Christianity is not monotheistic. However, people in non-Christian lands find it very difficult to understand how God the Father, God the Son, and God the Holy Spirit can be one God. Christians often answer that God can appear in many roles, just as one man may be a son, a husband, and a father.

The orthodox Christian is one who affirms the doctrines expressed in the great church creeds. Often the creeds have answered a Christian's questions before he ever had a real chance to ask them. Yet millions of orthodox Christians are still claiming to be satisfied by the answers of the creeds.

According to the orthodox teachings, God created the world and everything in it because of his love for goodness. He decided to embody goodness in the universe, in all living things, in everything that exists. This is a difficult doctrine to understand, as are all attempts to explain the very beginnings of creation.

Orthodox Christians say that once God had created men and put them on this earth to live, he would not leave them without knowledge of his will. He would give them a continuing revelation of their responsibilities. He would make it possible for them to live good and satisfying lives. This is because of an important quality God has—grace.

The grace of God makes it possible for men to know God and his will for them in their daily lives. It makes it possible for people to shed their old errors and strive again after perfection, or at least betterment. God's grace has led to a possibility of "eternal life," or an eternal quality of life, that is not destroyed by the death of a person.

Most Christians insist that there is some kind of heaven to which faithful believers may look forward with confidence. They view this "paradise" in different ways, though churches have long cautioned their members not to wish for material rewards for what should be a spiritual endeavor. Many orthodox Christians have also believed in a personal devil, called Satan, and in some kind of hell or eternal torment for those who are not "saved."

The underlying causes of the belief in heavens and hells, devils and angels, and the like are only partially understood even now. None of these things may have any actual existence. Yet they all say something about human needs. They tell of the torment brought by feelings of guilt and of "lostness." They tell also of moments of inner peace that seem "heavenly."

Persons who do not find freedom and joy in the present tend to worry unduly about the past or the future. Often their disappointment and disillusion leads them to hope for a tomorrow that will solve the problems which presently trouble them. The intense concern about the "afterlife," which so many religious folk have felt, is not a sign of inner health and genuine faith in life's possibilities. Rather, it reveals a lack of real faith and confidence in life.

Some Christians have always insisted that heaven and hell are not places to be inhabited in some remote future. They are conditions of the mind and soul. People were intended to live at peace with God. Because they are so designed, doing God's will brings them serenity. This is heaven. It is not necessary to die to find it. In the same way, one who violates the requirements for peace with God is living now in hell.

What Is the Good Life?

To live at one's best is not easy. It requires effort and sometimes pain. It is not enough to be kind and helpful to others, to follow rituals of private devotion to God, and to be sorry for past shortcomings. Details fall into proper place for Christians who recall that Jesus said men must first love God and then their neighbors. The good life requires a whole recentering around a spirit of love. Only in this way can good acts and sincere devotion have meaning and purpose. Then life is complete.

Most Christians believe that a person may still make mistakes in his day-to-day living, even when he has recentered his life around an attitude of love. They call such mistakes "sins." Sins can vary in their seriousness from sins against men to sins against God. Most of the organized Christian churches have catalogued sins and the extent of their wickedness. Members are warned against committing sins and instructed in ways of obtaining forgiveness once they have been committed.

Living by warnings, guilt, and regret is very different from the creative living that some Christians have achieved. They have discovered that a good life does not come from memorizing lists of things to do and things not to do. It comes from facing each experience with confidence and concern. Then all contacts and experiences are religious. All life is religious. And we are true to the best we can be.

All of present-day manners and morals appear to be

built upon foundations of self-restraint and respect for others. Through wise and temperate living, a person builds good habits. Good habits are an aid to a good life. But thoughtful Christians remember that every new act demands a new decision. The good life is attained by choosing wisely, weighing what may be temporary values against enduring ones.

For centuries, Christians have believed that they could find a deep, lasting happiness by living a life of devotion to God and to others. A person's greatest opportunity is to seek this end. But Christians admit that there are many people around us whose lives do not seem to reveal this quality. Still, each person is offered the opportunity. God does not choose for him. Devoted Christians have chosen for themselves, saying, as Jesus said: "Thy will be done."

17. Paths to Salvation

I T WAS from Jesus that Christianity got its start and its name. Jesus, however, would probably feel himself a stranger in discussions of Christian beliefs. As Jesus had found, to his sorrow, people are often more eager to pay respect to a trusted teacher than to follow his example of courageous seeking. From the first century, Christians forgot or ignored most of what Jesus taught. Instead they clung to Jesus. They saw in him many things which he apparently never dreamed of claiming for himself. Christianity is not the religion of Jesus. It is the religion *about* Jesus.

The chief reason for the differences Christianity has shown lies in a simple fact: the world is not the same as it was in Jesus' time. Because the world changes, religions change. No religion stands still. Every religion goes through a process of growth and alteration so long as it is a living force among people. It takes into itself ideas, hopes, fears, and customs. As a religion changes people, it too is changed.

So Christians have been changed by their beliefs, and gradually the beliefs have been altered. Often the different beliefs have formed the basis for a new fellowship or congregation of people, who see in it a stronger hope for a better life. Thus Christianity is represented by many different groups, each considering its own way to be an important, and perhaps better, path to salvation.

The Roman Catholic Church

Roman Catholics trace their beginnings back to a conversation between Jesus and Peter, as reported in *Matthew* 16:17—19. In this passage, Jesus tells Peter that he is the foundation of the Church. Peter is God's deputy on earth, with power to decide between right and wrong and to forgive sins or withhold forgiveness. Roman Catholics say that this statement proved that Jesus established their Church.

They say that God made Peter the first Pope, with full authority over all Christians. The line of Popes has extended down to the present day, with each Pope receiving the authority that was once Peter's. Each Pope is the visible head of the Church. Christ is the invisible ruler.

To Roman Catholics, the Church is an essential part of God's plan for the salvation of men. God, out of His love and grace, established the Church to make clear and definite the means of man's redemption. This is the only reason that the Church exists. Remembering this, Catholic leaders, from the Pope down to the priests, have constantly sought to make the Church effective in even the smallest details of man's salvation.

Faith. The Catholic is not asked to understand the plan of salvation. He is not asked to understand God—indeed he cannot. He is asked to believe and obey. His belief and his obedience rest on one basic doctrine: that if God were an infinitely loving God, he would set up some definite channel for saving mankind. The Roman Catholic Church insists that this is exactly what God did when he sent Jesus, his son, into the world. Jesus, in turn, gave to Peter the "keys of the kingdom."

All men need to be saved because of their share in the original sin that mankind committed in rebelling against God. Catholics believe the old story of how God provided a way of salvation from the burden of sins. By suffering as he did for men, Jesus paid the debt men could never hope to satisfy. Jesus made it possible for all people to receive salvation.

The Beatific Vision. Salvation brings a person the highest happiness he can know, the Beatific Vision. This does not mean simply "heaven." While it takes place in heaven, it is actually the experience of coming face to face with God. Only after death is this possible. While one lives, there are only suggestions of it.

Here in the world, our knowledge is limited. We can see only parts of truth. But we are made to know God and to know wholeness, and only through this knowledge can we find deep happiness. The Beatific Vision brings full knowledge of Truth, through the vision of God. It is beyond understanding and interpretation, but Catholics are assured by the Church that it is the greatest blessing.

The Bible. The scriptures, like the ritual, of Roman Catholicism are usually in Latin. In recent years, translations into other languages have been allowed. The Roman Catholic *Bible* includes the familiar books of the *Old* and *New Testaments* and an additional section known as the *Apocrypha*.

Catholics revere the *Bible* chiefly because it contains the story of salvation. They believe that there are no errors or uncertainties in the *Bible*. However, most Catholics do not study the *Bible* personally. They are not expected to interpret it for themselves, since the Church teaches a meaning for most of its passages. It is far more important that a Catholic study the teachings of the Church than that he read the *Bible*.

The Sacraments. A Roman Catholic comes into contact with his Church most frequently through his use of the seven sacraments, which give him guidance and strength on the path to salvation. He thinks of them as symbols of God's grace, which is channeled through the Church. Roman Catholics do not claim that the sacraments are the only way to salvation. But they offer a safe and sure escape from eternal unhappiness and punishment to those who use them.

Usually a Roman Catholic receives the sacrament of *Baptism* in his infancy. It removes the guilt of original sin and any sins committed up to that time. The sacrament of *Confirmation* is given when he is old enough to understand. It bestows the blessings of the Holy Spirit, which help the person to renew his intention and courage to follow God's will, as interpreted by the Church.

When a Catholic marries, the sacrament of *Matrimony* confers God's blessing and approval upon the marriage and upon the children who may be born to the couple. The Church considers this to be so important that it refuses to consider as a marriage any ceremony other than its own. Roman Catholics are taught that marriage is the eternal and holy union of a man and woman for the purpose of continuing the human race.

The sacrament of *Ordination* is given to purify and dedicate men and women for service in the holy orders of monks and nuns and for the priesthood. The ordained person puts aside his daily concerns, including marriage and family life. This is the supreme task of a Christian. For those who are able to undertake its demands, it offers more opportunities for salvation than any other way of life.

Persons about to die receive the sacrament of *Extreme*

Unction from the priest. It grants forgiveness of their last sins.

There are two other sacraments, the *Eucharist* and *Penance*, which make available more frequent spiritual blessing. Each Sunday and on certain other days, Catholics are expected to attend a service called the Mass, which celebrates the *Eucharist*. It is an age-old rite of remembrance of Jesus' last meal with his disciples and of his death upon the cross as a sacrifice for men's sins. In it, the priest performs a twofold miracle on wine and bread, turning them into the blood and body of Christ, without changing their appearance.

Catholics believe that this miracle of transubstantiation takes place when the priest offers the elements to God, in re-enactment of the death of Christ. The priest then partakes of both the transformed bread and wine. Unless illness prevents, Catholics are required to participate in the *Eucharist* through receiving the consecrated bread from the priest at the altar rail at least once annually, during Easter season. Through the repetition of this religious drama, a Catholic believes that he is aided in his progress toward salvation.

Since none of the sacraments remove a human being's tendency to sin, a Catholic frequently needs to seek forgiveness of his recent sins. This is possible through the sacrament of *Penance*. Penance includes regretting the sin, confessing to a priest, accomplishing penalties assigned by the priest, and obtaining forgiveness from the priest.

Saints. The saints honored by Roman Catholics include the early disciples, some members of holy orders, and others whose faith and actions showed their full dedication to the search for salvation. Catholics believe that these saintly persons lived the life that leads to salvation so successfully that they can help others. Through prayer to the saint, through burning candles before his image, and through other acts of honoring his spirit, the Roman Catholic believes that he may obtain some of the saint's merit for himself.

Mary. Roman Catholics revere the mother of Jesus as "Holy Mary, Mother of God." They believe that she was extraordinarily honored by God when he chose her to be the virgin mother of his miraculously conceived son. To many Catholics, Mary seems nearer and more concerned

with their daily problems than either Christ or God, who
inspire worshipers with awe. They sometimes call her
"Queen of Heaven," and they ask her to pray for them,
now and at the time of their deaths.

The Church and History. The word *catholic* means universal or general in its effects on men. Certainly the Roman
Catholic Church has affected a large part of mankind. It
has spoken to millions of people whose chief desire was a
sense of comfort and certainty in a life ridden with distress
and doubt. To these it has been a beacon of hope and se-
curity for the life they live now and the life they expect
to come.

The Eastern Orthodox Christian Church

Students of cultures have long noted that great differences exist between peoples of the Eastern and Western
hemispheres. From its infancy, the Christian religion was
jarred by the differences. There were conflicts and disagreements that were partly political, partly racial, and
partly religious. Finally, in the eleventh century, the conflicts resulted in a break that has never been mended. The
Eastern and Western churches excommunicated each
other, each claiming to be the one orthodox Christian
Church.

Church. The Eastern churches have no pope. Each
church is part of an area known as a patriarchate, which belongs to a federation of patriarchates. Eastern Christians
believe that they are members of the only authentic
Church stemming directly from the work of the first Christians. They call it the "Holy Orthodox Catholic Apostolic
Church."

Creed. The Eastern churches have not changed the
creeds, but they do not interpret them literally. Roman
Catholics have concentrated upon the salvation available
through the death of Jesus. But Eastern Catholics have
been far more interested in his divine-human nature. Roman Catholics have tried harder to obey the teachings of
the Church. But Eastern Christians have tried harder to
feel at one with God. Other Christians have been occupied
with winning salvation for the next life. But Eastern Christians have sought a spiritual rebirth in this life.

Sacraments. The Eastern Orthodox Christians observe

seven sacraments. Like Roman Catholics, they consider the mass their most important act of worship but both the cup and the bread are offered to the congregation.

Priesthood. Priests are looked upon as necessary agents between God and man. A priest may be married, if the marriage takes place before his ordination. Monks, of course, take the usual vows of devotion, chastity, obedience, and poverty. From among the monks, bishops are chosen for each patriarchate. They are known as patriarchs or metropolitans. They are equal in rank, though one may be designated as honorary leader.

Worship. The formal and impressive services of worship are dear to the Eastern Christians. Their priests intone the words of the ritual in Greek, or in Old Church Slavonic. Churches are decorated with special religious paintings called *icons*—never with statues.

Scriptures. The scriptures are substantially the same as the *Bible* familiar to all Christians. Priests encourage their people to read the *Bible*, and all may interpret what they read.

Practice. The Eastern Orthodox Christian has usually felt that his religion demanded a change in his inner life. He has not felt that it asked great changes in society or governments. For this reason, Eastern churches have sometimes accepted governmental and social activities that Westerners have condemned.

Most of the Eastern Orthodox Christians are found in eastern Europe, in Asia, and in Egypt. Since they have not usually been interested in recruiting new converts, their religion has spread to the United States and other lands almost solely through emigration.

Wherever sincere Eastern Christians have gone, they have taken the quiet beauty and rich symbolism of their worship service and their churches. They have impressed others with their quiet, unhurried search for an inner life that surpasses the human and links them with the divine.

Protestant Christian Churches

The Christian Church was to split again. The opening wedge was driven by a young German named Martin Luther. Little did he realize that his actions on that day in 1517 would lead to the far-reaching Protestant Reformation. All he did was announce his wish to debate his reasons for condemning a highly publicized sale of "indulgences," which guaranteed forgiveness of sins.

It happened that the sale he condemned was offered by an official of the Roman Catholic Church and approved by the Pope. And Luther himself was a priest. His announcement nailed to a church door was a startling challenge to the authority of the Pope and the Church, in a day when the whole of society was governed by their dictates. Faced with the demand that he retract his statements, Luther found that he could not do so honestly. His countrymen rallied around him, and the Protestant Reformation had begun.

Later leaders made other extensive "protests" against the authority of the Church. Their motives varied, but all of them had one belief in common. The way to salvation was not exclusively linked with the Roman Catholic Church and the Pope. Most of the protests were against the church system, not against the doctrine. For most Protestants, there are still no radical doctrinal disagreements.

There are now scores of different sects in Protestantism, with no single authority over them all. Most Protestants believe in the rights of others to choose their own religious beliefs and their own religious fellowships. Freedom of belief and choice of church have led to many variations on the Protestant theme. Despite this, Protestants are finding increasing areas of agreement, in their creeds and in their social-service efforts.

Salvation by Faith. Most Protestants claim that no person, regardless of what he does, can earn salvation for himself or anyone else. Salvation is a gift of God. One must believe that Jesus' life and death enabled people to regain a harmonious relationship with God. God's greatest blessing lies in this plan of salvation, which is open to all. All that is required is faith.

Dedicated Living. The religious life does not require that a person leave marriage, family, and daily human interests. Protestants have almost no monks or nuns, and their ministers are usually men with families. Faith, not works, constitutes the path to salvation. Faith does not depend on one's occupation, but God does call a person to give of his best efforts wherever he is. Religion is not a matter of church-going and pious meditation. It is the way you live each day.

The Priesthood of All Believers. Each person can go directly to God for himself. The task of the Church and its ministers is to teach men, not to act for them or command them. This is the real core of Protestantism. There are different reasons for the existence of the Church: to interpret God's will, to foster a fellowship of mutually helpful members who seek the same goals. Church governments vary, some being directed by ministers, some by ministers and designated members, and some by the entire membership.

The Bible. Most Protestants believe that the *Bible* contains the rules for faith and practice of religion. Protestants therefore study their *Bibles* seriously, reading them in their own language. Although many Protestants are now interpreting the *Bible* much less rigidly, there are still some who claim for it full authority, to the smallest word, without regard for its historical meaning.

Worship. Protestants are encouraged to pray sincerely and frequently. To some, prayer is a method of asking God for things. Or it is a way of helping friends from a predicament or "converting" someone. To the most thoughtful, it is an attempt to see things for what they really are, to come into a right relationship with oneself, with one's God, and with one's world.

Most Protestants observe two sacraments, baptism and communion. They do not believe the doctrine of transubstantiation. To Protestants, a person's feelings and intentions when he takes a sacrament are more important than the rites of the sacrament. This is also true of other religious duties, which include an offering to support the church, attendance at services, and participation in the Christian fellowship.

A Protestant is free to live the best and most dedicated life he can, choosing the fellowship in which he feels most able to do it. For help in living this way, some Protestants lean in faith on Jesus as their personal Savior and the Savior of all who believe. Others gain inspiration for the religious life from the noble example of Jesus' life.

Evangelical Protestants. The majority of Protestant churches are known as Evangelical Protestant churches. These groups have stressed their separation from the Roman Catholic Church, contending that such authority is a perversion of religion. The original protests were sincere and effective, but later each denomination developed an authority of its own not vastly different from what it had condemned.

Evangelical churches claim to support the orthodox doctrines. Chief among these are man's need for salvation and God's plan for man's salvation. In the first half of the twentieth century, there has been a renewed emphasis upon the old doctrines, in what is known as the neo-orthodox movement.

Some Protestant sects have claimed that certain teachings are fundamental to Christianity. Especially do they stress the complete truth of the *Bible* and all the miracles it reports. These Christians are called Fundamentalists. They are known for their strong emotional attempts to convert others to their faith.

Liberal Protestants. From the very beginning of Christianity, there were some thoughtful persons who saw that not everyone could be satisfied with the same words and the same experiences. Modern Christians who insist on freedom of belief have a well-founded tradition in the past of their religion. They are called the Liberals—a minority group in Protestantism. Slowly but steadily their number grows. Perhaps even more significant is the fact that their influence helps, little by little, to liberalize the more orthodox groups.

The true Liberal believes that each person must have an opportunity to grow in religious experience and understanding and to experiment with better ways of living. He believes that religion is for the whole person, both his feelings and his reason. He supports a church as an institution that helps people mature as individuals and as members of a democratic fellowship. The salvation the Liberal Protestant seeks comes through living life in its wholeness.

Christianity is not any one path or church or group. Christianity is what Christians make it. It is like a river continually flowing toward an unseen sea. The streams that flow into it are sometimes brackish. The eddies that form along its edges may sometimes stagnate. But, like all the other major religions of the world, Christianity continues toward a future no one can fully predict. With it go the hopes and aspirations, as well as the fears and anxieties, of the many millions who call themselves Christians.

18. A Religion to Live By

RELIGION at its best fills basic human needs. In the final analysis, all of us seem to need the same things. We need to feel that we are important to those around us. We need to feel that we have a place among our fellow men. We need to feel a purpose and a sense of direction in our lives. And we need to feel that we are moving toward our highest goals.

In every year since Jesus spoke and walked in the paths of Palestine, some people have found answers to their deepest needs in what he said and did. It matters very little that their disagreements in what to believe have often outnumbered their agreements. The important thing is that they have lived more richly because of Jesus' life.

Christians say that Jesus' message is timeless, because he drew teachings directly from the experiences of people he knew. To them, many of his statements are as true today as when he uttered them. Numbers of devoted Christians have been inspired to thoughtful living by his parables or by his Sermon on the Mount. Studied carefully and used thoughtfully, such teachings still bring peace of mind to present-day Christians.

Respect Yourself

Many of the people whom Jesus knew had lost a sense of their own true worth. They felt that they were not important to God or to men. The priests and religious teachers had only added to their problems by labeling them "sinners" and "unclean." To such troubled people, Jesus preached a message of confidence. "You are the salt of the earth!" "You are the light of the world!"

Sometimes loss of self-respect causes a person to cringe before someone else who seems to be important. There have been many over-humble Christians who have fol-

154

lowed the dictates and directives of leaders in their churches. They have not dared to doubt, to question, or to investigate, for fear they would make further mistakes. But nowhere in Jesus' message is there a reference to the right of some to dictate beliefs to others. Jesus issued an open invitation to people to join him in the search for the abundant life. In this search, all are equal.

We live today in a world filled with anxiety. This condition is produced by human beings, and it could be eliminated by intelligent human efforts. We worry about countless things—losing something we have, wanting something we lack. We are anxious about big things and little things, and our worries penetrate every part of our lives. We become increasingly unable to do the things we should and could do, because we are worrying so about the things we cannot do. Jesus tried to still such fears by pointing out real values.

Do not worry about life, wondering what you will have to eat or drink, or about your body, wondering what you will have to wear. Is not life more important than food, and the body than clothes? Look at the wild birds. They do not sow or reap, or store their food in barns, and yet your heavenly Father feeds them.

Now, as in Jesus' time, people can become emotionally and physically sick when they no longer respect themselves. Sometimes the sickness takes the form of contempt for personal desires, or feelings, or appearance. Jesus never ceased to encourage a person to respect himself. He knew that a person does not reach maturity unless he is able to accept himself as he is.

If one of us hates very much the way he acts or the way he looks, he will see only what he dislikes about himself. Is this a true picture of what he is? Indeed not. In the same way, some persons fail to get satisfaction from contacts with other people. They are thinking about appearances and manners of their friends, instead of really knowing them.

Jesus taught people that they should love their neighbors in the same way that they love themselves. If we are to love other people, we must first love ourselves. We have often been told to love ourselves last. But if this were the case, we would never love anyone. Loving oneself wisely is the basis of loving others well.

Love Other People

Too many people mistake possessiveness for love. They attempt to persuade the loved one, to make decisions for him, or even to act for him. Real love, said Jesus, consists simply of granting the person the right to be himself.

Now and then we try to make someone over or reform him. We usually learn that this destroys friendship. The more we try to force people into our pattern, the less influence we have with them. Force defeats itself. Love and acceptance are the greatest powers. They draw love and acceptance in return.

This is the hardest lesson of parenthood. Of course, babies must be protected from the possible danger their immature decisions might bring. However, as the years go by, parents must learn to let their children assume increasing responsibilities for their own lives. No one can become mature unless he is allowed to be himself.

There is a well-known saying, "I will forgive but I won't forget." A person "makes up" with the friend with whom he has quarreled, but he still cherishes secret resentments. These hurt feelings buried under the outward forgiveness have a chance to grow and fester. They prevent richer relationships with others.

Jesus was apparently well aware of the fact that if one does not truly forgive, he himself cannot be happy:

If you forgive others when they offend you, your heavenly Father will forgive you too. But if you do not forgive others when they offend you, your heavenly Father will not forgive you for your offenses.

And in the familiar prayer based on Jesus' suggestions to his followers, there is this request: "Forgive us our trespasses, as we forgive those who trespass against us."

Jesus was always reminding people that forgiveness was just as important to the wronged person as to the person who had committed the wrong. Forgiveness must be given as often as it is needed. There must be no limit to it. Otherwise, resentments will creep in and gradually prevent the unforgiving person from living happily.

Jesus taught that love was the law for all areas of human life, between friend and friend, between members of a family, and between groups of people. Christians have disagreed radically among themselves as to the application of this teaching. Some say that it cannot be applied to the relationships between groups of people and nations. They have even said that it is a "counsel of perfection," not intended to be followed by anyone on this earth. Some Christians have been able to bless wars, torture, and executions in the name of their faith. Others have insisted that love is to be applied in all phases of one's life, to the greatest possible extent.

Be Honest

Only when we have learned to love can we be honest with ourselves and with others. To Jesus, inner honesty was of first importance in living the good life. He called for people to be good, not just to practice goodness. He was distressed by pretenders who stood up to pray in the synagogues or on the street corners so that people would think them pious. Jesus said that the prayer said in the privacy of one's own heart and home was far, far better than a prayer for its public effect.

He told his followers that they would get nowhere in the spiritual search by repeating "empty phrases." How distressing it is sometimes that many Christians of today think that religion consists of repeating creeds and prayers which mean nothing to them. The real danger is that this dishonesty blinds us to our need for something more, and we go along trying to pretend that we are satisfied.

We are dishonest in other ways. We do good deeds to impress people favorably, without feeling the goodness. We learn polite words to say, without feeling the politeness. We join organizations and social groups, but we do not learn to love people more. We wear these fine false faces in public, and often we fool even ourselves. But the feeling inside is much more important than what we show on the surface. It is only when our inner intentions match our outward acts that we live abundantly. This is being honest.

Be Teachable

The person living at his best is one who is still searching for better ways to live. Such a person has kept his ability to wonder about life. He expects every day to teach him something new and better. He is open-minded and open-hearted, like a little child filled with wonder and delight at every new experience.

Jesus found that many "religious" people, like the Pharisees and the Sadducees, were not teachable. They felt that they already knew all the answers. So there was no need to raise the questions. Everything was settled according to the "Law" or the "Book." Life could teach them nothing new. It only made them certain that their answers were the only answers.

Countless Christians have learned the values of being eager to learn more. They have gone on examining their lives steadily and with concern. They have refused to accept the answers of someone else without trying them out. They have tried to follow this suggestion made by Jesus:

> Ask, and what you ask will be given you. Search, and you will find what you search for. Knock, and the door will be open to you. For it is always the one who asks who receives, and the one who searches who finds, and the one who knocks to whom the door opens.

"Blessed are those who are hungry and thirsty for uprightness, for they will be satisfied!" This is a prescription for religious living that has been applied and recommended by Christians as far apart in time as Francis of Assisi, Meister Eckhart, and Rufus Jones.

Because of petty problems and unimportant concerns, we often fail to see how generous life has been with us. It is a marvelous world in which we live. No one can take from us the basic, simple joys of living—the taste of food, the scent of pine trees in the rain, the beauty of a moonlit night, the sound of a waterfall, the colors of a sunset, the joy of loving and being loved. That is to say, no one can really take them away from us, except ourselves. Life's tragedy is not simply the inhumanity of man to man, in the form of concentration camps, exploitation, and wars. Life's tragedy is also the torture that we impose upon ourselves because of our failure to accept what is ours.

Life is a gift. "Freely you have received," said Jesus; "freely give." All of the fundamental joys of life are gifts that come to us without our having earned them. Most of us remain unaware of this too much of the time. Jesus often emphasized the wonderful gifts that life offers.

There is real significance in his parable of the prodigal son, the young man who wasted everything life had given to him, until he was "living on husks." To many Christians, this parable has said: You may have wasted everything life has offered you so far. You may be living on the husks—fear, anxiety, guilt, and resentment. Even so, the gracious life-giving forces are still at work in the universe, and in you, to restore you to your true self. The climax of Jesus' parable is when the harassed young man "came to himself."

Any one of us can come to himself, for each moment renews our opportunity. As long as we live, we face the challenge of continuing to grow mentally and emotionally. There for us all the while, said Jesus, are the richness of life and its resources for our deepest happiness. The Christian who meets his opportunity finds for himself the truth that Jesus spoke. "Behold, the Kingdom of God is within you."

ISLAM

19. Mohammed Speaks for Allah

FIVE TIMES a day, devout Moslems everywhere turn their faces toward a small city in Saudi Arabia. Kneeling upon a prayer rug, they pray facing Mecca. Often they use a prayer they call the *Fatihah*, which is as well known to them as the Lord's Prayer is to Christians:

> Praise be to God, the Lord of the worlds!
> The compassionate, the merciful!
> King on the day of reckoning!
> Thee only do we worship, and to thee do we cry for help.
> Guide thou us on the straight path,
> The path of those to whom Thou hast been gracious; —
>   with whom thou art not angry, and who go not astray.

These millions of people are following the Moslem ritual of prayer, laid down some fourteen centuries ago by Mohammed. This is one of the ways in which they show that they agree with what he told his people. Allah, God, is the first reality of their lives. Devoted Moslems can repeat from the Koran sincerely: "Verily, my prayers, and my devotion, and my life, and my death, belong to God."

Many years have passed since Mohammed lived, instructing his followers in what God required of them. But Moslems follow as closely as they can the commands of the Koran, convinced that it contains exactly what Mohammed said. They believe that what he had to say in the sixth century still provides suitable answers to their modern questions. What is God like? What am I? What is my responsibility to God? What will happen after I die? What is the right way to live?

Mohammed's Vision

In the darkness of one night in the year 611 A.D., a man of Mecca was keeping a lonely vigil of prayer and meditation in a cave in Mount Hira, just outside the city. Those who knew him well would not have been surprised, for he often retired to this cave for the solitude one needs for deep thought. But this one night—known by Moslems ever after as the "Night of Power and Excellence"—was to bring to Mohammed a new experience.

Suddenly he was aroused from his thoughts by an amazing vision. The angel Gabriel appeared, speaking God's command that Mohammed must call his people to the worship of Allah, the one God of all the world. Overwhelmed, Mohammed spoke of his inability to do such work. In answer, Gabriel repeated the commandment of Allah twice more. Mohammed fled from the cave to the mountain peak, trying to see if the night air would make the strange experience fade away. Even here, he heard a voice which told him that he was the Prophet of God.

Confused and afraid, Mohammed rushed home to tell his wife, Khadijah, what had happened. Could he be losing his mind? Khadijah reassured him, comforted him, and encouraged him to rest until he was calm again. She thought over the things he told her about that night. She added them to what she knew of her husband's life. And, quietly, she began to believe that the vision was true.

Mohammed, the Respected Citizen

Khadijah had long believed that her husband was an unusual man. Since the early days of their acquaintance, when Mohammed's uncle, Abu Talib, had recommended him to her as a caravan leader, she had respected his judgment and his character. He had accomplished his duties with success, and respect had developed into a mutual affection. They had married, although she had been a wealthy widow of forty and he only twenty-five. Their marriage of fifteen years had been a happy one, despite the deaths of their two infant sons. Mohammed was devoted to her and to their four daughters.

Khadijah knew that the men of Mohammed's tribe, the Koreish, agreed with her high estimate of her husband. They knew him as a thoughtful person, given to long periods of silence. They had come to respect him for this, and they often asked his advice when they needed an unprejudiced opinion. He had seemed always slightly different from the people who knew him, from his days as an orphaned child until now. Even as a shepherd boy for his uncle, watching the sheep in the vast and empty spaces of the desert, he had pondered the eternal questions of life and death. When his marriage had released him from the necessity of working, he had begun to take those questions out to the cave for lengthy meditation.

Khadijah, especially, knew the extent of Mohammed's dissatisfaction with what he saw of the lives of his people as he watched them in their dealings with each other. He had seen innumerable tribal conflicts in which the opposing parties hid their own selfish interests under labels of religion and honor. He had seen them as they traded and celebrated near Mecca, especially during the seasonal fairs, drinking, gambling, and dancing. He had even seen other Arabian fathers bury unwanted infant daughters alive, following a widespread custom. He had watched his people become so absorbed in petty tribal interest that they were unaware of the dangers from aggressive foreign countries.

Most carefully, he had observed their worship at the Ka'aba, the religious shrine in Mecca. Twice a year, the pilgrims came from all over Arabia to offer prayers and gifts to images of their three hundred sixty gods, one for every day of the Arabian year. The square stone building, the Ka'aba, still exists and still shelters the Black Stone, believed to have fallen from Paradise. Arabian legends told how Abraham and Ishmael had built the Ka'aba, putting the Black Stone (a meteorite) into its corner. Mohammed had watched the pilgrims there and in the marketplace in Mecca, where they could buy small idols to take home with them.

What he had seen of Arabian religion had left him full of questions and doubts. He had contrasted Meccan worship with his memories from caravan trips to other lands and with what he had learned from Christian, Jewish, and Zoroastrian visitors to Mecca. What of the Zoroastrian beliefs in a Day of Judgment and the punishment of sinners? Most Arabs lived without regard to where their lives were taking them. What of the sacred books of the Christians and the Jews, which told of revelations God had made to prophets? The Arabs had no revelations to help them.

They had never had a prophet. What of the single God that other peoples worshiped? Arabs gave homage to three hundred sixty gods. Mohammed had pondered these differences for a long time.

The Unpopular Prophet

As Khadijah remembered all these things, she was sure that Mohammed's vision had to be true. From the first, even before Mohammed himself was fully convinced, she believed that her husband was God's chosen prophet. Her unwavering belief helped him to believe in himself. Soon other visions came to him, giving more details of his mission for Allah. For three years he waited and meditated and spoke of Allah quietly only to relatives and close friends. At the end of that period he had gathered about him a small circle of just thirty followers. The time was ripe for more active work.

Soon he was speaking to small groups of people in the marketplace, in the streets, and in the Ka'aba. He told them that they must give up the worship of their many gods and goddesses and follow the will of Allah, the one God of all the world. If they did not do so, they would suffer dreadful punishments after the Day of Judgment. At first the people listened curiously, for this was a man they knew and respected. When Mohammed continued in his strange sermons, they began to laugh and mock. That they should abandon their old ways of worship was unthinkable. Had not their fathers and their fathers' fathers worshiped in the same way? The gods and goddesses whose images were in the Ka'aba had always looked after them. Their old rituals and customs were familiar and comfortable. What did they know of Mohammed's one God?

Some of the tribe began to doubt his sanity, and others became uneasy at his derision of the worship of the idols in the Ka'aba. They made their living by caring for the needs of the pilgrims who came to Mecca for worship. If people did what Mohammed asked, the source of their income would disappear.

Despite growing objection, Mohammed persisted in telling what Allah had revealed to him. He warned his hearers to listen well, for these were the final revelations that God would make to men. Before all things were created, there was a book in Heaven which contained all truth, Mohammed told them. Part of what the book contained had been revealed to Jews and to Christians through their prophets, including Jesus. But the biggest part of it was being revealed to Mohammed.

Finally the Koreish could stand it no longer. They refused to listen. They began to disrupt his preaching and persecute his converts. They tried every means to discourage him from his task. Since they would no longer listen, he began to talk to strangers in town for trade or pilgrimage. The Koreish warned travelers about him, but their warnings only served to whet the travelers' curiosity. Visitors carried home stories of this strange preacher, who spoke in defiance of the members of his tribe. Some visitors from a city named Yathrib were especially impressed with what Mohammed preached to them. They were looking for a leader who could help them overcome the effects of a disastrous war between two tribes. They began to think that Mohammed might be a good choice for the responsibility.

At the height of the persecution, Khadijah died. Her death was followed by that of Mohammed's influential uncle, Abu Talib, who had been his protector, though never his convert. These two losses, added to the increased persecution, troubled Mohammed greatly. He was beginning to doubt that he could ever accomplish his goals in Mecca, where even the safety of his growing band of followers was threatened. These circumstances led to his decision to accept when the citizens of Yathrib invited him to become their leader.

The Escape to Medina

The departure from Mecca had to be carried out with great secrecy, or the enraged Koreish might do them harm. All the two hundred followers were sent on ahead. Mohammed and a long-time disciple, Abu Bekr, left at the last moment. Despite all the dangers, the whole group got safely to Yathrib. In honor of the arrival of their new leader, the people changed the name of their city to the "City of the Prophet." It is now known as Medina. The movement of the Moslems to Medina is called the Hegira, meaning flight or exodus. It was made in 622 A.D., and that year became the first year of the Moslem calendar.

Mohammed was now in a position to exercise great power. He became ruler and priest, lawgiver and judge, prophet and commander-in-chief for the whole community. He drew up a constitution for his people, trying hard to unite the different groups into a close-knit fellowship. The people were to help each other against all enemies and in all difficulties. They were to abide by the decisions of Allah, as revealed to his prophet, Mohammed.

One of his first acts upon reaching Medina was to construct a simple mosque for the center of the Moslem worship. He preached there frequently. His sermons described simple but firm moral codes of kindness to travelers and loyalty to friends. He urged that they pray often and be faithful in acts of devotion to Allah. In the language of the desert, Mohammed told of rewards for righteous living and punishments for a wasted life. Paradise sounded like an oasis, while hell was a place of heat, thirst, and loneliness.

The Triumphant Prophet

Mohammed had always confidently expected that Jews and Christians would accept him and his message as the next chapter in a book of revelations that they all held in common. Thus, when he went to Medina, he was prepared to be very patient in his efforts to win over the Jewish citizens to the new Medina agreement. He even asked his followers to pray facing Jerusalem, and he emphasized the common elements in their traditions.

However, it soon became apparent that the Jews living there had no intention of calling Mohammed their prophet. A good many of them even ridiculed his revelations. Relationships took a turn for the worse when some of the Jews violated the terms of their agreement with Mohammed. The prophet then issued a demand that they either join in Islam or leave the area. The order was carried out by Mohammed's armies. It was the first of a long list of Moslem victories over opponents. Moslems have always claimed that such moves were necessary to protect the development of their religious community.

Actually, this marks an even more important point in the history of Islam. Mohammed had begun to see that his prophecies were not going to be accepted readily by non-Arab peoples. Islam gradually was directed more and more to Arabs. Jewish and Christian traditions were minimized and Arab traditions stressed from then on. Moslems were no longer to pray toward Jerusalem. They were to face Mecca. And Mohammed and his followers looked with increasing eagerness toward the time when they could go to Mecca once again.

As the fame of the prophet spread throughout Arabia, more people became converts to the new religion. Finally, Mohammed felt that it was necessary for the welfare of his followers that he take Mecca with his armies. So, eight years after he had barely escaped from Mecca with his life, he re-entered it as a conqueror. As always, he was generous with his foes, forgiving most of them. They had only to confess their faith in Allah and in his prophet.

Mohammed went immediately to the shrine. He stripped the idols from the Ka'aba, declaring it a place for the worship of Allah. Mecca became the holy city of Islam.

The fall of Mecca caused many other communities to declare their submission to the prophet's religion and rule. For some time Mohammed had been convinced that his chief mission was to unify the Arab tribes by bringing them together into a nation governed by the will of Allah. When tribes did not pledge their allegiance, they were put to the sword and overcome in holy war, which the Moslems believed represented the will of Allah. Gradually the far-flung tribes united into what was to be the nation of Arabia.

To keep a promise he had made to the faithful, Mohammed went back to live in Medina. But he made pilgrimages to Mecca, and he always looked upon that as the rightful center of the worship of Allah. On his last pilgrimage, he preached a sermon that was to be one of his best remembered. In it, he declared that all believers were brothers, and as such must ceaselessly help and respect each other.

Mohammed's Gifts to Islam

Not long after his return to Medina from that last pilgrimage, Mohammed died. He was sixty-two years old. Much had happened since he had sat alone in the cave near Mecca and thought of the meaning of life. Allah's message had been given and received enthusiastically. The Arabs had turned from idols to the worship of Allah.

They no longer fought, tribe against tribe. They were all brothers. They no longer danced and drank and gambled in riotous celebrations. They prayed and fasted and felt the presence of Allah close beside them.

The legacy Mohammed left to his followers was very great. He left them united and strong enough to resist foreign aggression. He left them a faith which they found clear and satisfying. He left them a zeal for that faith that led them to prescribe it for all other people. He left them trained disciples to carry on the movement. He left an army capable of spreading Islam to other lands in holy wars. He left them the example of his life, which had been fully devoted to the will of Allah.

Abu Bekr, who had often assisted in services, was a natural choice for the prophet's successor, or caliph. And, after a short period of mourning, Islam went on as before toward the realization of all the prophet's dreams. History was changed. People were changed. They were changed not alone through experience with the man Mohammed but through the creed he taught them. It is the creed that millions of Moslems still follow, declaring with complete faith: "There is no God but Allah, and Mohammed is his prophet."

20. Moslems Hear and Obey

MOST modern world religions became organized religions by an accident of history. In many cases, their roots are buried so deep in time that we cannot know the incidents that helped them to develop. But Islam was distinguished by two facts from the start. First, it became a religion as the result of deliberate planning and well-considered efforts. Second, its whole development took place after world history had begun to be carefully recorded.

In a short span of years, Mohammed had lifted himself to a unique position of leadership among his people. He had had the time and the opportunity to plan thoroughly to meet all the social and spiritual needs of his fellow men. Mohammed, convinced that he spoke for Allah, had given rules for beliefs, for religious duties, and for proper conduct. As a result, Moslems found themselves with a guide to almost every activity or situation undertaken by human beings.

What Must I Believe?

Somewhere along in life, every thoughtful person wonders about the power or force responsible for the creation of everything that we see, hear, smell, taste, and touch. What kind of power or force is it? When and how does it operate? What caused it to operate in the first place?

Mohammed had faced these wonderings as a young man. Through his visions, he believed that he had found the answers. He unhesitatingly recommended these answers for everyone else. Allah, the Eternal, is the source of all creation. The central confession of all believers is belief in Allah: "I bear witness that there is no God but Allah."

Allah is just and merciful. He sees and hears everything. His presence is everywhere. He knows all a person's acts, good or evil. On the Day of Judgment, Allah judges the lives of men. In the beginning, he ordained the way all things should have their existence. In the end, he determines eternal destiny.

Mohammed believed that the world, in its orderliness and dependability, told the story of a personal, purposeful God. Allah had created all things and had predestined all events. Yet men can reach him through prayer, and men are free to work out their own lives. However, they must know that the consequences of paradise or hell await.

Since Allah long ago removed himself from active direction of his creation, it might be difficult for men to know how to do his will. But Allah understood man's need. He established three ways to reveal his will to men: a prophet, the Koran, and the angels.

The first of these ways is expressed in the second part of the Moslem statement of faith: "I bear witness that there is no God but Allah, and Mohammed is his prophet." Moslems respect other prophets—including Adam, Noah, Abraham, Moses, and Jesus. But Mohammed is the last of the prophets, the "seal." No other prophet ever spoke with such authority. No other had such a complete revelation from God.

Mohammed never claimed to be more than an ordinary man. His chief quarrel with Christians was that many of them worshiped a Son, as well as a Father-God. This was an addition that he could not tolerate. "There is none in the heavens or the earth but comes before the Merciful as a servant."

> God the Eternal,
> He is God alone!
> He begets not and is not begotten!
> Nor is there like unto Him anyone!

Mohammed's revelations have been preserved in the Koran for the enlightenment of all succeeding generations. The Koran is a particularly significant book to Moslems because it is identical with another book which many Moslems believe has existed in Heaven since the beginning of time. In this heavenly book, the will of Allah is recorded. The same revelations contained in it are the ones given to Mohammed and written in the Koran. The Koran is God's whole message to men.

Orthodox Moslems have never doubted that the text of their sacred book is correct. "Memorizers" learned the things Mohammed said. Soon after his death, his words were written down in a single copy. This made it possible for Moslems, almost from the start of their religion, to have a sacred scripture.

The third means of knowing the will of Allah is through angels. To Moslems the most important is Gabriel, known to them as the "angel of revelation." It was Gabriel who brought Allah's messages to Mohammed. Gabriel and the other angels surround the throne of Allah, in the "seventh heaven" of paradise, doing Allah's will and ministering to his decrees.

Another angel—or really an ex-angel—is the Devil, who was banished from heaven because of his pride. Moslems believe that he is in charge of hell and, with his assistants, works to thwart the will of Allah by tempting men into evil ways. However, Allah is all-powerful and all-determining. So the Devil's work is limited to what he can do in the framework of Allah's plans. The Devil can never really thwart Allah, for Allah's plans include letting the Devil do his work of temptation.

God is just, but life does not always offer rewards and punishments in accord with the quality of a person's living. Must not the good be rewarded and the evil punished? The Koran tells Moslems that a Last Judgment will come at the end of this age and the beginning of eternity, when Allah will judge all souls. Each will be tried on the record of his life. Allah is merciful, and a good person's reward is greater than he deserves. But punishment for evil will be exactly what the sinner merits.

Those believers who have followed the will of Allah will be eternally rewarded by residence in paradise. The Koran's description of this heavenly dwelling sounds like a magnificent oasis, with flowing waters, refreshing beverages, fruits and fowl, and youths and maidens serving the needs of the residents. Thoughtful Moslems believe that the real appeal of paradise is the eternal presence of Allah.

Hell has been prepared for those who decline to submit to the will of Allah. Again, the description is one such as a desert-dweller might imagine. The damned suffer eternally in fire and heat. What they eat and drink is like boiling water. When they call for aid, that aid becomes a further torment. Some Moslems say that the Koran is using picturesque language to describe the total lack of joy in existing without Allah's presence.

Allah, the prophet, the Koran, angels, and the Last Judgment—these things a man must believe. There is a sixth

essential belief: in Allah's complete power and boundless-
ness. Actually this is a repetition of some of the characteristics of Allah, pointing out the necessity of utter obedience on the part of men. A man does not need to understand the will of God—in fact, it is impossible. But he
must submit to it. "I hear and obey" describes the relationship of man to God.

The name *Moslem* means "submitter," while *Islam*
means "submission to Allah's will." Moslems believe that
submission brings peace and fulfillment. They object to
the terms "Mohammedan" and "Mohammedanism"
because they imply a worship of Mohammed. Moslems
worship only Allah.

What Must I Do?

Part of Islam's rapid spread across the world was due to
its simplicity. The creed is clearly stated in six beliefs, as
we have seen. The religious duties of believers are just as
clearly stated in five requirements, which are known as the
"Five Pillars" of Islam.

Declaration of Belief. First, a Moslem must declare his
faith and pledge his loyalty. "I bear witness that there is
no God but Allah, and that Mohammed is the prophet of
Allah." Spoken before witnesses, this declaration can admit a new believer into the fellowship of Islam.

Prayer. The chief religious discipline of the Moslem is
prayer. Mohammed named five times a day for formal
prayer, and he encouraged private prayer as a continual
practice of the presence of Allah. At sunrise, at noon, in
mid-afternoon, at sunset, and at nightfall, Moslems are
called to prayer. From the minarets, "pillars" of prayer, the
call floats out to millions of devoted Moslems:

> Allah is great, Allah is great . . .
> There is no God but Allah.
> Mohammed is Allah's apostle.
> To your prayers! To your devotions!
> Allah is great; there is no God but Allah!

First, there is the ritual of cleansing and the placing of
the prayer rug. Then the Moslem kneels down, bowing
in the direction of Mecca. The prayer often takes the form
of a renewal of submission to Allah's will. Often it is an
expression of praise. For some it is a recognition of the

fact of God's constant presence. This last most nearly
meets the wish of Mohammed, who hoped that all believers might know Allah as the real experience of life.

Moslems try to be in a mosque for prayers whenever possible. These simple buildings are designed so that the worshipers face Mecca. All decorations are of geometric de-
signs, in accordance with Mohammed's insistence that no
images be made. Fridays are special days for public prayer
in the mosques. Men who go to the mosque perform the
cleansing ritual, perhaps gather about in groups to hear
readings from the Koran, and then participate in the prayer
service. In each mosque, a leader directs the public worship and gives weekly sermons on Moslem beliefs.

Usually the congregations are made up of men, most
Moslems believing that women should worship at home.
Mohammed himself declared that such private devotions
were better for women. If they do attend the services,
they are usually seated behind screens.

Fasting. Fasting is a frequent religious act of devout
Moslems. There is one fast that is necessary for all believers, except those excused for physical conditions or special activities. This fast occurs during the month of Ramadan, the ninth month of the Moslem year. During the
fast of Ramadan, food and drink may not be taken between sunrise and sunset. Moslems believe that fasting is
a good reminder to put spiritual things first. They try to
read or hear the whole Koran during the month and to be
in the mosque often.

Almsgiving. Belief in the brotherhood of all Moslems
has helped to continue an early custom of sharing their
goods and money with the needy. For a time, sharing was
legally required in the form of a yearly "tax." Now it is
often paid in the form of a voluntary pledge, to help the
needy and to support Moslem schools and mosques. Although a person may choose not to pay it, very few do.
Their friends expect it, and they believe that their generosity to others will bring Allah's generosity to them.

Pilgrimage. Every Moslem lives with one dream and
expectation for this life uppermost in his thoughts. That
is the pilgrimage to Mecca, a city so sacred that non-
believers are not admitted. Annually, during the twelfth
month of the Moslem calendar, the paths to Mecca are
choked with pilgrims. They hurry to join in the ceremonies
centering around the ancient Ka'aba and the Mosque of

Mecca. Mohammed urged his followers to make the pilgrimage every year. Now, due to the wideness of the Moslem fellowship, each person is asked to go once a lifetime. While there are many who are never able to make the trip, it remains the life goal of most Moslems.

Once arrived, the pilgrims enter the sacred bounds of Mecca, each wearing a garment designed to make all Moslems, rich or poor, appear the same. Rank and race and wealth forgotten, the pilgrims join in the sacred rituals of the pilgrimage. They fast and thirst all day; they dramatize traditional legends; they honor the Black Stone in the Ka'aba. Having made the pilgrimage, the Moslem is forever after a respected person among his fellows.

The pilgrimage has been an important unifying agent for Islam. Mohammed probably emphasized it because he expected that it would serve the cause of unity among the Arab tribes. It still helps to strengthen the bond of fellowship among Moslems.

What the Moslem Owes to Others

For the guide to his daily living, the Moslem has to look no farther than the Koran. A large part of the fuel for the fires of Mohammed's inspiration was the immorality and lack of worth-while purpose in the lives of his fellow men. The Koran is filled with messages reflecting this concern. Other religions may develop people who live apart from others, putting their personal desires and needs second to a search of the spirit. Islam does not try. Islam tries to make men fit for living with each other.

Long ago Mohammed forbade gambling and intoxicating beverages to believers. Probably, at the time he did so, he was thinking back to the scenes of riot and revelry at the seasonal fairs near Mecca. If the rules against gambling and intoxication caused a change in the lives of his followers, even more so did his statements in regard to women. Men who had been able to divorce and marry wives at will were asked to consider women as creatures of the same Creator, with rights of their own. Husbands must respect wives' rights to their own dowries and must abide by certain rules on divorce and remarriage. Mohammed urged every effort to prevent a divorce, for nothing else was so displeasing to Allah.

Americans are often startled by the Moslem practice of

polygamy. The Moslem, according to the *Koran*, may take four wives. (Mohammed at one time, through Allah's special permission, had ten.) However, Mohammed asked that men examine their circumstances and their temperaments very carefully before they did so. If they could not treat all equally in care and affection, they should have only one.

More and more Moslem men are marrying only one wife, either because it is what they believe or what they can afford. Many Moslems now try to understand the spirit or intention of the laws of the *Koran*. The more liberal believers assert that monogamy is in the spirit of the *Koran*. They realize that times have changed since Mohammed make the laws about wives. Then the proportion of women to men was greater than now. Moreover, according to the old tribal customs, the only way a man could aid a poverty-stricken or widowed woman was by marrying her.

Although Mohammed's life and work insured to the Moslem woman many privileges she had not enjoyed before, she still was expected to be retiring and modest. Her religious acts were better done in private. It was more fitting that she keep to the seclusion of her home than that she flit about. She was not to be hidden from all eyes, but modesty and quietness were her most becoming qualities.

In earlier days, Moslems owed a responsibility to their brothers to fight if necessary. Mohammed said that a war of defense was permissible, but that one must attack only when fighting for Allah. Such holy wars spread Islam over a large portion of the globe in a very little time. Mohammed taught that Moslems must be gracious to the conquered, bearing no hostility.

Actually, all the rules about the way a good Moslem lives his life stem from one of the last things that Mohammed said to his followers. During his last sermon at Mecca, he made the famous declaration of the brotherhood of all believers. Stronger than family ties even were the ties of the brotherhood. All believers were sacred and all men equal in the sight of Allah. For this reason alone, kindness and respect were due to parents and children, to slaves, and to all others.

Moslems must be faithful in their promises to each other. They respect each other's lives and property. The measure of a man's goodness is the way he acts toward his brothers. All a man believes can be told from what he does, as this Moslem proverb shows: "No one of you is a believer until he loves for his brother what he loves for himself."

Today, when people have long been accustomed to living as nations, social responsibility is well known. But the Arabs of Mohammed's time had spent their days in constant, petty bickering and fighting among tribes. Mohammed was saying that a person's responsibility was not limited to those who lived in his town or belonged to his tribe. He was responsible for his share in the welfare of all those who had values, interests, and goals in common with him.

Mohammed had enlarged the concerns of his people, turned their gaze outward to the rest of the world, and helped them to fit themselves for a place in the world. All this was done in the short space of twenty years. The average Moslem learned his lesson well. The Moslem who follows the prophet's teachings about brotherhood is a good citizen in the world.

21. The Brotherhood of Islam

During Mohammed's life, disagreements among his followers were largely discouraged because of the unifying effect he had upon them. But upon his death, his people—like people everywhere—discovered that there would be some lack of accord in carrying out the rest of the goals of Islam. There was some discussion in the beginning about the person to take Mohammed's place in leading the faithful. It was settled without much difficulty with the selection of the trusted Abu Bekr as caliph. Unfortunately, succeeding vacancies in the caliphate were not to be filled so easily. As the Moslem empire grew, so did disagreements.

There were several groups with definite ideas about the best method of selecting the caliph. The Companions, who had been Mohammed's closest associates, thought that the caliph should be one of their number. Some thought that the leadership should stay in Mohammed's family. The Koreish thought that they, as the tribe of Mohammed, should have control of the caliphate.

The Spread of Islam

Under Abu Bekr the Moslems attacked Syria in the first holy war against a foreign country. The Moslem conquests had begun. Under the second caliph, Omar, Moslem armies marched in other wars which were eventually to bring into the Moslem fold parts of Africa and India and all of Mongolia and Spain.

The most dramatic chapters in the history of Islam were written about the fierce warriors who streamed out of their Arabia into conquest of the world. Devout Moslems claim that they did so in a sincere effort to save the whole world from the Last Judgment. The prophet had made them feel that it was their mission, and if necessary they would force the world into this salvation. Force was almost always necessary. It became customary to offer three options to non-Moslems—acceptance of the Koran, the

176

payment of a special tax for the privilege of remaining non-Moslems, or lastly the sword. Primitive as were their equipment and supplies, the Moslems continued to win, inspired by their conviction of a mission and by other less religious reasons. By Moslem law, the soldiers could keep four-fifths of the booty won in a holy war. If he survived, a soldier could become very wealthy. If he died, he had won direct entrance into paradise.

Others explain that part of the Moslems' interest in widespread conquest lay in the fact that their existence up to now had been limited to the boundaries of their own infertile desert land. Before them now lay the riches of land and of culture of the fertile and prosperous Mediterranean civilizations. Not only the produce of the land attracted them, but treasures of science, art, and philosophy as well.

It was during this time that the treasury in Medina began to reach the bursting point. Who had ever dreamed of such riches as were pouring in from the conquered countries? And the caliph was in charge of the way it was to be spent. To many, it became a matter of utmost concern to be able to share in decisions concerning the selection of caliphs. The lives of a good many caliphs were sacrificed to the ambition and greed of some unscrupulous groups.

As Islam became widespread, including more and more non-Arabs, agreement became difficult and at last impossible. For centuries, however, the more orthodox Moslems insisted on one religious leader for the whole Moslem world. But times and situations had changed and were still changing. Finally in 1924 the caliphate came to an end.

During the early years after Mohammed's death, questions were raised which resulted in a major division among Moslems. This division has lasted until today. Both groups consider that their way of thinking and acting is in close accord with the revelations of Mohammed. Both groups believe that their movements represent the correct development of the Moslem religion.

The Sunna

The orthodox or conservative branch of Islam is known as the Sunna, so named for its emphasis on a collection of Moslem traditions called by the same name. Sunnis believe that what is contained in the Koran and in the Sunna define the limits of beliefs and actions for Moslems. The Koran tells the word of Allah. The Sunna tells of actions and sayings of Mohammed and of early customs of Moslems.

For a time, the Sunnis believed that the Koran and the traditions must be interpreted exactly as they were written. An honored teacher named Ashari helped the Sunnis to develop slightly different beliefs, which would allow the use of reason in interpretation. He explained some of the seemingly contradictory beliefs by saying that Allah was all. Allah had created everything and all acts, and therefore Allah was responsible for both good and evil. Men must accept that, without debating about whether it is possible.

Some had wondered how the Koran could be eternal, as Mohammed had taught them. If that were so, would that not be setting up something else alongside of God? And was not the worst sin of all the worship of more than one God? Ashari taught that the Koran in the form that Moslems have is not eternal. But in the form in which it first existed in the mind of Allah, it is eternal.

There are always some people who are not chiefly interested in ritual or religious law or in theology. There have been many Moslems of this temperament. Some of them began to express their faith in ways they saw among people of other religions. They felt that religious truth was not confined solely to creeds and rituals. Truth could be gained from direct communion with God. And so some began to practice the meditation and other devotional exercises of the mystics.

At first they must have been greeted with raised eyebrows, since they were going beyond the usual religious practices of the Moslems. Like some self-denying members of other faiths, they put on uncomfortable wool robes and paid no attention to their physical and social needs. They were dubbed Sufis, meaning "wool-wearers." As their number increased, they began to gather into brotherhoods, emphasizing utter devotion to God. Their goal was union with Allah in this life, not waiting until after death.

The Sufis gradually gained respect from orthodox Moslems. One of the first to understand the worth of their path to God was Ghazzali, a Moslem teacher who has been called "restorer of religion." Ghazzali watched the mystics in their devotions and himself became a Sufi. He saw the value in the life of complete devotion.

He began to teach a modified *Sunna* theology, based largely on Ashari's doctrines, but including the mystic's emphasis on loving devotion. He believed that a person was not a believer in a religion until he had felt a religious experience. A religion has to change something about the life of a believer. Without this change, a person was only on the surface of religion, not at the heart of it.

Real religion was arrived at through three steps. First of all, a person must feel sorry for his past sins. There must be a need for a change. This is repentance. Then a person must center his life around God, seeing that nothing is important but this devotion. Then the believer must strive to live a life free from sin. The Pillars of the Faith will help him in this. And the disciplines of the Sufis will further help him.

Ghazzali's chief target in Islam was the emphasis upon reasoning as the only method for learning God's will. He said that people must be always ready to give obedience to Allah, whether they understand or not. Although Ghazzali formulated his teaching late in the eleventh century, it is still the final authority for Sunnis.

The Shia

About one-fifth of the world's Moslems belong to the non-conforming, unorthodox group called the *Shia*. Principally located in Persia, the Shi'ites trace their beliefs back to the prophecies of Mohammed and to the Koran, too. However, the main thing dividing them from the Sunnis is their belief in a tradition that Mohammed left the guidance of the faithful in the care of his cousin and son-in-law, Ali. Ali, they say, was the divinely appointed leader, the Imam, of the Moslem community. The leadership of Islam should have centered in Mohammed's family. Shi'ites believe that the three caliphs preceding Ali held the caliphate unlawfully and in disregard for Mohammed's wishes. For this reason, may Shi'ites curse these men in their daily prayers.

Shi'ites have honored the descendants of Mohammed by making them religious—and sometimes political—nobility. Each sect has named certain of these descendants as the divine Imams for each generation, believing that each of the Imams was infallible and sinless. The sects have not always agreed about who was Imam and when. Neither have they agreed upon just when the line of divinely appointed Imams ended.

Some of the Shi'ites believe that the last of the Imams did not die. He went into hiding and he will reappear just before the Last Judgment. Until that time, some Shi'ites are confident that the "hidden Imam" will appoint representatives on earth, in order that the people may have his guidance. The Shahs of Persia (Iran), who claim to descend from the seventh Imam, are supposed to be the representatives of the "hidden Imam."

The Shi'ite sects have survived the long centuries of their disagreement with the larger number of Moslems because they have clung persistently to their beliefs. Sometimes they have survived persecution by appearing to conform, while carrying their beliefs "underground." Modern Sunnis are inclined to be tolerant toward these unorthodox Moslems.

Any religion that attracts the loyalty of a large number of people is bound to accumulate prescribed creeds, rituals, and customs. Soon there are those who see that such organization has come to preoccupy the believers, so that the original inspiration and purpose have been forgotten. Sometimes these observant ones start a movement to purify the religion of the externals and get back to the fundamental faith.

Such a purifying movement was launched in Islam in the eighteenth century. Some of its effects still linger. The people who supported it had become distressed at the increasing tendency to revere important teachers and theologians, even Mohammed. They felt that this was coming very close to worship of several gods. "Get back to Allah and to the Koran" was their passionate advice to Moslems. The movement attracted support in Saudi Arabia, where historical markers were removed from the graves of Mohammed's family and other central figures.

Changes in Islam

Almost in spite of itself, Islam has changed somewhat from its original course. For a time, change in Islam was considered to be evil. This is the religion that for years forbade the translation of the Koran from the Arabic because Allah had given it in Arabic, and it must not be altered. But changes have come.

Countries of the Near East have become increasingly interested in modernization, industrialization, or Westernization—call it what we will. Today most Moslems feel their first loyalty to the country where they live, rather than to the whole Moslem brotherhood. These facts of the "shrinking" of the twentieth-century world have forced Islam to become more tolerant of other beliefs and less brittle about its own creed.

Two forces, however, have worked in the opposite direction. One of these is the creation of Pakistan in India, the outgrowth of Moslem-Hindu bitterness. In two parts —one to the west of India, and a smaller section to the east—Pakistan is an interesting experiment in the relief of religious conflicts. The emigration of Moslems into Pakistan has made them increasingly conscious of differences between Islam and other religions.

The other force counteracting change has been the creation of the Jewish state of Israel, with the accompanying movement of thousands of Arabs out of the area where their homes had been. Moslems were highly displeased with the decision. Whenever people have an enemy in common, they stress the other things they share. Thus, Moslems have re-emphasized their beliefs and customs.

Contributions of Islam

The world long ago became accustomed to what the Arab Moslems had done to it. World history was changed when the first Moslem armies marched against Syria. Despite the complaints of the conquered, Moslems brought forces for good. Wherever they went, they furthered the arts and sciences and medicine. They kept order and morality in society.

Those who accepted the Allah they worshiped came to revere a God of dignity and majesty—ever ready to be approached by the lowliest of men. For truly, in Allah's eyes, no men are lowly. All are equal. The brotherhood of Islam has not stopped at boundaries of nation, race, or wealth. For Moslems believe that the eyes of Allah do not see the senseless differences sometimes imagined by men.

All this stemmed from the inspiration of a man of Mecca who felt a responsibility to lift his people up from the worship of idols to the worship of the one god, Allah. Toward the end of his life, he looked out over his followers and prayed: "Oh Lord! I have delivered my message and accomplished my work."

Moslems answered with their voices then and have answered with their lives ever since: "Yea, verily, thou hast."

CONCLUSION

22. Toward Richer Living

HAVING started an acquaintance with these different great religions of the world in the preceding chapters, you may be asking: "Out of all these religions, must I individually choose my religion? Must I decide whether to be a Buddhist, or a Hindu, or a Moslem, or a Confucian, or a follower of Judaism, or a Christian?" Perhaps, on the one hand, you have been happily surprised to find these other religions much finer than you had supposed. You may even have felt that you have discovered a few new and deep insights which your own religion seems to have missed. On the other hand, you may have been worried over the possibility of accepting a belief that others would call "Buddhist" or "Confucian" lest you become a kind of outcast in your church or community. It's a comfortable feeling to believe that one's own culturally given religion is the best of all religions—at least for oneself.

After all, you say, there are certain things that life gives us without our choosing. By accident of birth, each of us is white or brown, a blonde or a brunette, an American or a Frenchman, a male or a female. Other "givens" are sociologically determined for us—our country's mores and our family or national religion. By accident of birth, each of us is born into a culture that calls itself by some special name, such as Hindu, Buddhist, Jewish, or Christian. Long before we have reached what is called the "age of discretion," when presumably we can make our own choices on the basis of reason and nationally interpreted experience, most of us have become so thoroughly saturated with culturally engendered values that few of us ever make a radical decision to break with our upbringing.

Most of us, however, have a deeper need in addition to our readiness to follow the past or to be like the people around us. Beneath our apparent activities and interests lies the seed of desire to discover for ourselves who we really are and what in life is important. No matter how

184

many millions have asked these questions before us, and no matter how sure they have been of their answers, each one still has a private yearning to go exploring for himself. This is true of the infant who has just learned to crawl and who applies the "mouth test" to everything he touches. It is true of the young person who is trying to discover the meaning of life, love, and work. It is true of the older person who has not lost his capacity for sustained wonder.

It is important that we keep alive within us this desire to search and question. There is more faith in honest doubt than in all the unexamined creeds of past and present. In this sense each of us must articulate his own religion—that is, his own concept of what is of supreme worth in living, his own mode of expressing that concept, his own commitment in daily life to the values he believes to be basic. (The particular words he uses to describe these processes are relatively unimportant, as all liberal spirits in religion have everywhere recognized—to the consternation of the cautious conservative or reactionary priest.)

Strange as it may seem, it is only when we discover the depths of personal experience that lie beneath the differences that we are able to appreciate why there are these differences. And what we find at the deeper levels shows us the universal elements. We discover that in deep ways all people are much alike—even though each one is an original.

Space for Living Creatively

One of the perpetual wonders in life is that there is always room for another person, another idea, another explanation. Each of us has a chance to fill a place in our universe. We build a "life space" for ourselves first through our attitudes and then through our efforts and actions, with our neighbors and in our total world.

On the one hand, we may try to wrest a "life space" for ourselves by taking an attitude of hostility toward others and by moving aggressively against those we think stand in our way. Or, on the other hand, we may shy away from the opportunities life offers and retreat into a private world bounded by fear and suspicion. In both cases we shall have settled for a small, restricting place in life.

But we have a third choice. We may greet each person

and situation we face with confident, friendly, inquiring attitudes. In this way we absorb more and more of what people and situations offer. Thus we construct a constantly enlarging "life space." Life seems to offer its richest rewards to those who have developed the capacity to "stretch" their "life spaces" continuously. It is true that no person can wholly make his surroundings, but each person does build a personal environment of attitudes and feelings which may significantly modify his surroundings.

We Can Help Each Other

Each of us to a degree constructs his own "life space." Yet like the warp and woof in a woven rug, our "life spaces" overlap or interpenetrate. As the English poet, John Donne, expressed it long ago: "No man is an Iland, intire of itselfe; every man is a peece of the Continent, a part of the maine." In improving the quality of our own "life spaces," then, we cannot help improving the quality of others'.

Each of us can learn most from the other by following the principle of "the mote and the beam." By becoming aware of "the beam" in our own religious or irreligious eyes, we are less inclined to concentrate on seeing "the mote" in the other fellow's eye. But to look for the worst in the other person's faith while concentrating on the best in one's own is fatal to human fellowship and larger community. Rather, we must look for the best while not ignoring the worst. From Hinduism and Buddhism, for example, many Westerners can come (and have come) to a new understanding of the importance of the search for the real self. To do this one need not forget the shortcomings of Hinduism as pointed out by a Hindu like Gandhi. Nor does one need to learn how to sit cross-legged and eat rice off banana palms while wearing a *dhoti* or a *saree*. Nor does one need to repudiate what one enjoys in his own tradition. This open-mindedness probably will not involve a change in one's religious affiliation, institutionally speaking, if one is fortunate enough to belong to a group that believes in permitting the widest measure of honest seeking to every member.

Indeed, it is quite possible that a person could learn just as much about the importance of self-knowledge through a deeper study of the ignored aspects of his own religious tradition as through the study of another religion. But in a world filled with people who have so little appreciation of the best that other cultures have to offer and so great a tendency to defend their own cultures or religions, there is a practical argument for trying to enter into the mood or spirit of other philosophies or religions. In this process many people have discovered that for the first time in their lives they have really experienced a widening of horizons and an extension of self-knowledge. They have also gained a deeper appreciation for their own religious tradition.

In this sense, any religion or any culture, thoughtfully studied, can become a kind of multiple mirror through which each of us learns to see himself more fully. Each of us is an individual, and yet each is a part of a larger community. In so far as we are individuals, we must go into the depths of our own experiences to find the meaning of life. No parent or teacher or great religious leader can do that for us, though the community may furnish us with clues and guides. Each of us has this inalienable right to a direct relationship to the universe. But each must attain it for himself.

The tragedy is that too many of us remain content, even in our adult years, with the answers or descriptions offered by someone else. We limit ourselves to what others say instead of re-exploring the basic questions for ourselves. Many of us cling to the values emphasized by some past leader without exploring their meanings in the present. Almost all of us have closed off certain areas of thought somewhere along the line.

There are doors to be opened, and each of us can help himself and others in this door-opening process. What other people are, what they say, and how they say it can all be helpful in the opening of doors. Knowledge of the past is worth-while to the extent that it helps us open doors in the present.

Toward the Discovery of Our Oneness

In the light of the approach to life which we have been discussing in these chapters, certain types of attitudes, beliefs, and actions are ruled out. What attitudes are ruled out? Those reflecting an uncritical reliance on other peoples' experiences or words, whether from Orient or Occident; attitudes of fear and submissiveness, as well as attitudes of cocksureness or a "know-it-all" approach; attitudes of coercion or the feeling that there is "an only way" of going about the important experiment of finding life's meanings.

What types of beliefs are excluded? Beliefs that build walls around oneself or around one's tribe, shutting out an honest concern about why other people believe what they do; beliefs that persist because our underlying guilt feelings or anxieties are stirred thereby; beliefs that stress one's shortcomings at the expense of one's virtues or potentialities; beliefs that cramp one's spirit, stifle one's courage or morale.

Similarly, certain types of actions are ruled out. To use an "Inquisition" or to persecute in the name of religion is the very denial of man's humanity as well as proof of how stunted one's own faith is. In every religion childish attitudes and ceremonies can be found. But like childish attitudes held by young people or adults, they cannot be legislated or forced out of existence; they must be outgrown. Most people need sympathetic help in learning how to outgrow their blind spots, or in evaluating childish religious actions and attitudes.

There is a practical corollary to this that should affect the work of every society with a "missionary" dream. Attempts at conversion too often become forms of coercion. It is well to try to see the best in the other person's religion even while by example one is seeking to share his own faith. By example alone is one's personal religious faith given eloquent testimony in a way that respects the integrity of the other person's worth.

To permit each of us to grow to his fullest stature, we must move out of that kind of competitive atmosphere which sees the diversity of religions as "a battle unto the death." Most Orientals have learned to resent "Occidentalization" in matters of religion; similarly most Occidentals would resent "Orientalization." All of us must become teachable citizens of One World. Our primary allegiance must be to that pattern of divinity as it emerges in all things human; our secondary allegiance can then safely be given to that culture, society, family-system or nation that has been as a friendly guide to us on the road to an affirmation of humanity's true oneness. "Divinity is round us—never gone"—this is the lesson we must be constantly learning.

INDEX

Abraham, 109, 162, 169

Abu Bekr (disciple of Mohammed), 161, 164, 167, 176

Abu Talib (uncle of Mohammed), 161, 164

Ali (Moslem leader), 179

Allah (God), 160ff, 168ff

Amitabha (Amida), 70-72

Amos, 112, 127

Analects (stories of Confucius), 87

Ancestor reverence, 93

Arabs, 115

Arhat, 67-68, 70

Asceticism, 51

Ashari (teacher), 178, 179

Atman, 28-29, 30ff, 43, 44, 59

Avatar, 41, 44, 45

Beatific Vision, 146

Benares, 42, 51

Bhagavad Gita, 22

Bodhisattva, 70ff

Book of Judgment, 119, 120

Bo-tree, 66

Brahma (creator), 27

Brahman (God), 27ff, 30, 34, 40ff, 64

Brahmanas (rules of worship), 22

Buddha, 48ff, 51

Buddhism, 48ff, 60ff, 66ff, 102

Buddhists, 44, 62, 64, 127

Burma, 67

Caliphate, 176ff, 179

Capernaum, 129, 131

Caste, 32-33, 45, 65

Ceylon, 67

Ch'an (Zen) Buddhism, 73

China, 67, 76ff

Christianity, 108, 126ff

Christians, 22, 27, 44, 126ff, 165

Chuang-tse, 79ff, 82

Classics (Chinese), 87, 90, 95

Clinging, 55

Confucianism, 86, 87ff, 102

Confucius, 76, 78, 87ff

Conservative Judaism, 116, 118, 125

Cow-worship, 42

Craving, 56ff

David, 109, 130

Day of Judgment, 163, 168, 170, 176, 180

Deuteronomy, 111, 122

Donne, John, 186

Durga, 41

Eastern Orthodox Church, 149ff

Eckhart, Meister, 158

Esther, 123

Evangelical Protestants, 152-153

Exodus, 109, 110, 124

Fatihah, 160

Filial piety, 92

Five Constant Virtues, 89ff, 93

Five Pillars of Islam, 171ff

Four Noble Truths, 54ff

Francis of Assisi, 158

Fundamentalists, 153

Gabriel, 161, 170

Gandhi, 33, 42, 44-45, 46, 186

Ganges, 42

Gautama, 49ff

Genesis, 109, 110, 122

Ghazzali, 178-179

Goddess of Mercy, 71-72

Golden Age, 78, 87, 90

Gospels (New Testament), 126ff

Great Epics, 22

Great Purification, 101

Hanukkah, 122-123

Hatred, 61-62, 132

Hebrews, 108ff, 138

Hegira, 164

Hillel, Rabbi, 110

Hinayana, 67ff, 74

Hinduism, 22ff, 186

Hindus, 22, 127

Hindu trinity, 27

Holy Eight-Fold Path, 60ff

Holy Spirit, 141

Hosea, 127

Hymn of Creation, 26-27, 28

Imam, 179

Insect-Hearing Festival, 99

Isaac, 109

Isaiah, 109, 111, 121, 160

190